DEAR HYWEL
FROM AVIAD

SELF-NAVIGATION:

A Compass for Guiding Your Life and Career

To Hywel —
With my warm
wishes and appreciation
for your friendship!
Kim Barnes

B. KIM BARNES & AVIAD GOZ

A Johari Press Publication JOHARI PRESS

ISBN: 0615679781
ISBN-13: 9780615679785

Advance Praise for Self-Navigation

"So many people around me could benefit from better navigating their lives! This book is definitely a great help. I am considering making it a must-gift for anyone turning 40!"

Pascale Demont, consultant and coach, Biviers, France

" In times of crisis, it is extremely important to know what we want to be. Fathom your desires without being blinded, select the best options, take action without getting lost. This very pragmatic but profound book can help us to make the right diagnosis and to find our way."

Clotilde Renard, organizational consultant and coach, Paris, France

"There is no greater need for people working today in a context of great change than practical tools to help them navigate. Aviad and Kim are two world thought leaders who offer us a way to personal transformation…to feel more clarity, motivation, confidence and focus. Enjoy the journey…"

Peter Nankervis, Knowledge Director of Lighthouse Australia, Sydney, Australia

"The concept of self-navigation is one that can change the life of a person when completely understood. This book will be of tremendous help to people who really want to change the default choices that have led them to a different life from the one they want. Un grand bravo to the authors."

George Stoleru, organizational coach, Paris, France

"This navigation guide is the creation of two world-famous organization development consultants and executive coaches. They bring a no-nonsense approach and tools along with real stories to illustrate the challenges and consequences of decisions we take today for our life and career satisfaction tomorrow. Reading this book is a great investment in your future."

Robert Rogowski, learning and development executive, Edinburgh, Scotland

"The book is incredible, really smart and helpful... It explains the situation you are dealing with, shows you the complexity of the road ahead, and asks/guides you to come up with your own answers...The book states that your choices are your path to greatness, and then ... shows you a clear path through questions and strategies that help you find your own way and develop your own reusable system ...Thanks for a book that teaches you how to fish!"

Sharon Mulgrew, strategic learning consultant, Emeryville, California

Dedication

To Roni and Don, without whose support this book would not have been written, and to the many coaches, consultants, friends, and clients who have taught us how to navigate. We are especially grateful to our friends and colleagues who took the time and care to review and upgrade the manuscript along the way:

Pascale Demont
Galit Moskovich
Sharon Mulgrew
Robert Rogowski
Beverly Scott

Contents

Preface: The Story of Jane

When I met Jane eight years ago, she was feeling miserable. From the outside, it seemed she had everything that should make a person happy and satisfied. She had a successful career as the head of a department of speech therapy in a famous health center. She was happily married to a loving and supporting husband and had two charming children. Yet she complained about her situation and said that she needed a profound change.

I tried to understand why she needed such a change. Her income was high; she was recognized as an expert and had high status among professionals in her field. The future looked certain; she could go on working there until retirement. Even her work hours were comfortable; she was able to spend quality time with her family. Jane could clearly see how all the years of work and investment in her career had led her to this point—she knew that many people might envy her, but she felt trapped in a golden cage. She had no passion for what she was doing.

I asked what she would like to do instead, and she was not sure. She just had a feeling that she was in the wrong place at the wrong time. After some deep discussions about what did excite her interest, it became clear that Jane was passionate about making high-quality, healthy food—something she did as often as possible for family and friends. She felt that this was how she should be using her time and talents. In trying to work out a "practical model" that might be suitable for her, she came up with the idea of starting an organic goat cheese operation and running a farm.

This was miles away from anything she had ever done. Still, she was convinced that it was the right direction for her. As part of our discussion, I suggested that Jane enter a "time machine" to explore her dream—to spend time at a farm like the one she wanted to create. I explained that this would allow her to see if the reality of living her dream or vision would match her expectations. Because of our conversation, Jane attended a two-week course focused on making organic dairy products. It was on a goat farm in Switzerland. She returned from the experience with great excitement, her eyes shining, and said, "Yes. This is it. This is what I really love doing."

It took two years to convince her husband and children to move away from the city, but eventually they bought a small farm and moved to the country. Jane learned everything possible about goat dairy products. After two years, with great pride, she sent me a photo of the first batch of organic cheese products that had gone from her farm to the market. Today, four years later, Jane is a successful organic dairy farmer.

Once the farm had proved successful, she opened a small, rustic, and romantic restaurant based on her products. Many people make the two-hour journey from the city to buy her products and eat in her restaurant. In our last conversation, Jane reported that she was very satisfied with the journey she had undertaken. She said, a little wistfully, "I should have made this move much earlier. I stopped myself because I feared losing my comfortable position. Now I am living the life I have always wanted to lead."

This life story and many others that I have been involved in caused me to wonder about the processes of change that people undergo in their lives and careers and about the choices they make. I researched many such stories and processes, and I eventually developed a system of navigation for individuals, teams, and organizations. The system is called N.E.W.S.™, and for the last ten years, it has been in use in many countries and organizations throughout the world. Our company, N.E.W.S.® Coaching and Training, based in Switzerland, has worked with leaders of Fortune 100 companies and small-business owners, with artists and designers, mayors and military commanders. Our clients have ranged from communities and teams to couples and individuals. This system has helped to transform the way people navigate their careers, guiding them to better and more satisfying lives.

Aviad: My co-author, Kim Barnes, and her company, Barnes & Conti Associates, have developed powerful tools for learning and improving interpersonal and thinking skills. Together, we decided that many more people could benefit from applying these systems and tools as they navigated their lives and careers. We agreed to combine our two approaches in the form of this book.

Kim: Aviad Goz and I have worked together successfully as global partners since 2007. Some time later, when he first showed me the N.E.W.S.™ model and material, I was immediately enthusiastic. I saw that he had developed a simple and powerful way for people to take control of the direction of their lives. Over the past few years we have discussed how we might collaborate and bring this to a larger audience. At some point, the idea of spending a week of intense work to begin writing this book in the middle of California's wine country emerged. We both navigated our busy lives in that direction and made it happen. The result was a creative collaboration – and a list of excellent restaurants and wineries for after working hours that we would be happy to share!

In *Self-Navigation*, we first examine how people make decisions. Then we introduce and develop the concepts of self-navigation and choice points. Following that, we focus on each direction and offer skills and tools for better self-navigation—tools that have been tested in many companies and with a large number of individuals across the globe. Throughout the book, we tell stories of people who have used the approaches portrayed here. Finally, we suggest some solutions that you can adopt and use to navigate your life and career in a better, more productive, and more exciting direction. For simplicity's sake, we will use the word "I" to refer to either author's experience.

Use this book as a general guide to self-navigation. It can also help you navigate through a choice that you currently face. It can be a useful tool for HR or OD consultants or for managers as they help others in the organization navigate their careers. Finally, it can be used as an introduction to the N.E.W.S.™ workshops and coaching process.

We wish you a great journey.
Aviad Goz
B. Kim Barnes

March 2012
Sonoma County, California

Section One
Self-Navigation

Chapter 1

How We Make Decisions

People like to think of themselves as thoughtful, rational beings. When they are confronted with a choice, they consider the options, weigh the alternatives, perhaps do a cost-benefit analysis, and then, based on the evidence, make the best possible choice to achieve their goals. Based on those assumptions, nineteenth- and twentieth-century economists who followed John Stewart Mill developed the theory of the "economic man." According to this theory, when supplied with the right information, we make decisions that are thoughtfully designed to fulfill our needs. This idea nicely suits our self-image.

However, while a simple observation of our own and others' behavior might have given us a good deal of evidence to the contrary, it took major contributions by behavioral scientists such as Daniel Kahneman and Amos Tversky,[1] writing in the 1970s, to point out that human beings use rules of thumb (heuristics) and

1   Daniel Tversky and Amos Kahneman, "Judgment under Uncertainty: Heuristics and Biases," *Science, 1974*

biases in making decisions rather than working everything out in a rational way. Among the many contributions that they and behavioral economists, such as Richard Thaler, Dan Ariely, and others,[2] have made in the past fifty years are the following tested conclusions. In decision-making, people tend to:

- rely on a single piece of information or on past experience to govern the decision process.
  Example: You find giving feedback very difficult, so you choose to avoid roles where you will have to manage people.
- place too much importance on one aspect rather than weighing all significant aspects of a situation.
  Example: You are attracted to the weather in California, so you take a job there without taking into account the higher cost of living.
- accept suggested reference points as an anchor for decisions or responses to choices.
  Example: You allow the price of a shirt in the first shop you visit in Bangkok to frame your expectations about how much you will have to pay for similar items elsewhere.
- ignore information that does not fit assumptions or expectations.
  Example: In a famous experiment, a large percentage of experimental subjects failed to notice a person in a gorilla suit strolling across a basketball court in a video they watched; they expected to be judged on the number of free throws they counted.
- strongly prefer avoiding losses to achieving gains.
  Example: You sell stocks as soon as the price starts to decline, rather than waiting to pick up more of it at a bargain price.

---

2   Dan Ariely, *Predictably Irrational: The Hidden Forces That Shape Our Decisions*, (New York: Harper Perennial, 2010).

- accept a situational frame that fits within their comfort zone and operate from that rather than from evidence that may contradict or fall outside of the frame.

   Example: In a famous case in Massachusetts, police arrested a black man for the murder of a white woman during an apparent carjacking in a black neighborhood. The real murderer turned out to be the woman's husband, who shot her as part of an insurance fraud plot; the arrested man had nothing to do with her death.

- bias their decisions based on suggestions made by those they admire or respect.

   Example: Not long ago, several followers of a guru died of hyperthermia after participating in a ritual that involved spending too many hours in a sweat lodge. Apparently nobody questioned the wisdom of this in time to prevent the tragedy.

These and many other biases and fallacies can govern the decision making of even the most educated and intelligent among us. Without a conscious and disciplined approach to analyzing and making decisions, we are likely to make poor estimates, money-losing gambles, and sometimes disastrous choices that affect our lives and the lives of others in very negative ways. Missing the gorilla on the basketball court is amusing; picking the wrong person out of a police lineup is a terrible mistake that could cost another person his or her life. Paying much more than the value of a shirt in Thailand might be embarrassing, but making the wrong choice of a spouse, despite all the warning signs, can lead to years of misery. Choosing which stock to buy based on a taxi driver's recommendation can be an expensive mistake. Choosing a career based on what your parents or teachers thought you should do can commit you to a dull life of dreams deferred and passions unfulfilled. Choosing to follow an expert who does not have your interests at heart or does not know what he or she is doing can be life threatening.

Life is full of opportunities to make choices and decisions. At times, we may feel that our options are narrow, restricted. At other times, we are overwhelmed by options. A Russian friend of mine, visiting from what was still the Soviet Union, found the number of kinds of cereal in an American supermarket so overwhelming that she felt paralyzed by the complex decision making that would be required and walked away with nothing. "At home," she said, "we would buy whatever was available. There was never a question of choice. Here, I don't know how to begin to make a choice among all of these boxes. I have nothing to go by." In this book, we hope to offer you a star to steer by, a way of guiding yourself through the maze of options as you reach the important choice points in your life.

Chapter 2

Choice Points

Throughout our lives, we arrive from time to time at choice points. From early in life, the choices we make set us off in a particular direction. We ask ourselves important questions at key moments: What do I want to study? Where should I go to school? Which job should I take? Whom should I marry? How should I raise my children? Whom should I choose as a successor? Should I take the promotion I was offered or move to another company? Should I stay with my familiar and comfortable corporate role or strike out on my own? When should I retire? What should I do next?

Each choice defines the next set of options we have to consider and leads to the next choice point. This is how we create our lives and careers—a stretch at a time, choice by choice. Some decisions lead us to dead ends; some open up amazing opportunities we might never have imagined.

Many things about our lives are determined by circumstances beyond our control: the culture, family, religion or set of values we are exposed to, the economic conditions we are born into, and the needs of the marketplace, the economy, and the people we are lucky or unlucky enough to have as teachers, mentors, or managers. In situations that are largely made up of preexisting contexts and conditions, we may have the choice only of acceptance or rejection of those conditions.

Victor Frankl, a psychotherapist and Holocaust survivor, developed his practice of *logotherapy* based on the principle that one always has a choice about how to feel and how to bring meaning to life, even in the darkest circumstances. He said that even in situations over which we have no control, we have the freedom to choose our attitude toward them. He called this "the last human freedom."

For example, Major James Nesmith, a prisoner of war in Vietnam, spent five years playing a completely visualized game of mental golf every day. This was his way of staying sane within an insane circumstance. He chose to use the time in a way that kept his intellect alive. He completed those grueling five years in good physical and mental condition. When he was released and returned home, he found he had improved his game by several strokes.

We encounter choices daily. Most of them we make by default: "I always buy that brand." "I am used to that system." If they don't work out, we can always change them. Problems arise when we use our convenient default programming to make major life choices: "Every oldest child in the last three generations of my family has been a lawyer, so I guess that is what I should be." "It would be too hard to start over at my age, so I guess I'll stay where I am." "It's time for me to have a child, and this guy seems nice enough, so I may as well marry him."

Upon reflection, you might discover that you have had a recurrent pattern of decision making, such as the avoidance of risk taking,

taking the path of least resistance, or perhaps the opposite: pursuit of the most challenging and adventurous route to your destination. This means that whenever you are at a choice point, you are likely to use the same code, thereby recreating the same situations and similar relationships or issues. We call these "default choices." A default choice is one that has been made according to an existing, predetermined code. The choice did not involve free or thoughtful consideration, but was framed and knowable in advance. Choices made by default often lead us into predictable pleasures and problems—but sometimes they can lead to unexpected and unwelcome consequences: boredom at work or in a marriage, loss of opportunities to express our real passions, forcing ourselves into molds where we really don't fit.

"Wouldn't it be great if…" is a phrase we often use in a sad or passive way, referring to a missed opportunity or deferred dream. What if, instead, we could use that phrase as a spur to action—to creating and believing in a meaningful direction or vision and then making it a reality?

Chapter 3

Navigation

The purpose of navigation is to locate one's position accurately, to set a target destination, and to progress toward that destination. Throughout history, we have developed navigation capabilities through many stages, from stellar navigation to compasses to gyroscopes to GPS systems based on satellites. We have always had a need to identify our location in order to set our course and direction. To contemporary GPS users, it seems simple and obvious; a friendly voice in their car directs them to unknown destinations with great ease. But throughout history, many ships, caravans, and travelers lost their way due to poor navigation and primitive technology.

The word *management* is derived from the Latin word *mano*, which means "hand." The Romans likened the act of management to the role of the driver's hand in controlling and navigating a chariot. To them, managing meant driving and navigating a vehicle toward its desired destination. Now we use terms such as "senior manager" or "director" to denote people who have the responsibility to navigate the organization in the best possible direction.

Individuals also have to navigate in the sea of uncertainty that surrounds them. Navigating oneself in today's uncharted water is a complex task, given frequent changes in the economy, in the workplace, and in social systems. To navigate your life effectively, you must begin with your current location. You assess what your situation is, examine many options, and then make decisions about the best direction and the next destination. You explore options, overcome doubts and fears, plan well, and execute with high discipline. That is successful self-navigation. And that is what this book is all about.

The act of self-navigation is a process that requires constant engagement and staying focused on the goal. You can't do it while on autopilot; your virtual GPS will work only if it is set to the destination you have chosen. Hands-on navigation, with your eye on the compass in the midst of change and ambiguity, has become essential for success. Every major decision about your education, career, relationships, or place of residence is an act of navigation that will influence the course of your entire life.

Following are some important principles for successful navigation:

- If you don't know where you are starting from, you will probably navigate from the wrong premise; you won't know how far or in which direction you need to go.

- If you don't know where you are going, you may end up in the wrong place.

- When you are very young, the navigation of your life is in the hands of others—your parents and teachers.

- True self-navigation occurs between puberty and old age and involves many choice points and decisions.

- Navigation is a lifelong process. When you give up choice and change, you give up on your life's journey.

- In the navigation process, you will come across major and minor choice points or crossroads.

- At each major choice point you create the next section of your life's path—for better or for worse.

- Thus, the major decisions that you make are crucial and require deep thinking, attention, and a good set of navigation tools.

The ability to self-navigate requires a certain belief system. It may be easier for those who come from more individualistic cultures or from families that allow and encourage independence in their children. To self-navigate, we need confidence in our decision making, a willingness to accept risk, and a belief that choices matter. A fatalistic, passive, or pessimistic attitude is antithetical to self-navigation. A popular trope from the last century was "not to decide is to decide." The unfortunate consequences of allowing others to make your decisions for you or to follow the path of least resistance are evident in many lives.

Some years ago, I was working with a group of senior executives in a national electric utility. They were each in charge of thousands of employees; they controlled budgets of many millions of dollars. This company was known for its tough, competitive organizational culture.

I had a conversation with the chief operating officer. Although it was early in the day, he looked exhausted. His shoulders slumped; his eyes were dull; he spoke in a monotone. I asked him how he came to this senior position, and he told me his story. He said that when he was young and looking for his first major job, he heard that one of the big banks was hiring. He set off for an interview, deciding to take the bus. At the bus stop, he met an older businessman who asked him where he was going. The young man said he was heading for a job interview at the bank. The stranger said that he knew that they were also recruiting in the national electric utility and that the young man should consider that option. On a whim, that young man decided to take a different bus and headed to the electric company's interview site.

This, the COO told me, was how he ended up working in the electric utility and not in a bank. From that point, things just rolled forward. At a major choice point, a casual comment by a stranger at a bus stop defined the course of his life.

Chapter 4

What About You?

We've discussed decision-making, choice points, and the concept of self-navigation. Take a few minutes now to think about your own life. Where have your major choice points occurred? What was your process for making decisions about which way to go? What or who helped you to navigate on your life journey?

As you review your life, consider whether there were important decisions along your path that you don't remember consciously making. Were there times when a decision was called for, but you did not make it? How did each of those decisions (they were, in fact, decisions not to decide) affect the next phase of your life? Is it possible that you made some decisions using a default pattern—that is, a sort of program you followed without thinking, so that you made decisions without being conscious of doing so?

Sometimes serendipity comes into play. You meet the right person at the right time; an opportunity comes along when you are ready for it; fortune seems to smile on you in the course of a particular day. At other times, you seem to be moving under a black cloud. Bad luck follows you—you are walking along the street just when a paint bucket falls from a platform, spraying you with a particularly ugly color. A passing pigeon targets you for a little gift. Your boss loses her temper with you while you are on the phone with a top prospect. The toddler sitting behind you on a long, crowded flight has a meltdown.

These experiences may be random good or bad fortune. On the onehand, many of them have to do with your own attitude and preparation—or lack of readiness. To what degree have you allowed chance to determine your life's course for good or ill? On the other hand, to what degree have you taken advantage of opportunities to move forward in ways that align with or promote the direction you have chosen? One definition of luck is "opportunity that meets readiness." That means that the more we are prepared, the better we can recognize the opportunity as it comes along.

Activities

1. Draw a line from the day you were born, stretching into the future. Mark today's date, then look backward from today. Mark the approximate dates when you made significant life choices. Label those choices, and if you can, recall the alternatives you were considering. Draw a dotted line leading from each alternative in a different direction from the direction you chose. Below each of those choice points, write some notes about how you made the decision. How long did it take you? What alternatives did you consider? Who or what did you consult to help you choose? How did you feel afterward? Looking back, how do you feel now about the decisions you made then?

2. As you reflect on the major choices you have made or the major crossroads where you have chosen a path without conscious attention to the process, what default patterns do you see?

3. How aware of these patterns were you at the time?

4. Being more aware now, how might you have chosen differently? What differences might that have made in your life?

5. How might being aware of default patterns in your past affect your future choices?

Chapter 5

The N.E.W.S.™ Navigation Model

The N.E.W.S.™ model is based on the assumption that each of us has a potential for greatness. When we speak of greatness, we refer to achieving the highest and best fulfillment of your own talents and skills—that is, becoming the most excellent *you* that it is possible to become. In his best-selling book, *Good to Great*,[3] Jim Collins states that the research shows that "greatness is not a function of circumstance. Greatness, it turns out, is largely a matter of conscious choice." In other words, you can fulfill your potential for greatness through making conscious, smart, ethical decisions at key points on your life's journey.

As we approach a major decision, a crossroad, or a choice point, we must assess where we are in order to know where we want to move. To do this, we need a reliable navigation system, a metaphorical compass, a guide we can trust. Such a system needs to address many complexities. It should be

---

3   Jim Collins, *Good to Great* (San Francisco: HarperBusiness, 2001).

- easy to understand and simple to use;

- flexible, applicable to many situations;

- useful and practical.

- structured and holistic, but compatible with other systems; and

- based on experience and evidence.

The N.E.W.S.™ model is designed to help you navigate through difficult situations, major decisions, and choice points in your quest to fulfill your potential for greatness. We hope it will assist you in achieving alignment, motivation, and focus by revealing your most important possible contributions.

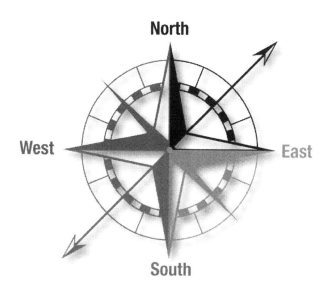

The word N.E.W.S. is an abbreviation of the four directions of the compass: North, East, West, and South. In this model, each direction represents an area for questioning and reflection. This model will reveal to you the work that you need to do and the type of development that will allow for the best navigation process. Using the N.E.W.S.™ model, you will analyze your current situation and then implement a set of tools designed to enhance self-leadership and navigation.

- In the *North*, we ask a simple question: *Where do you want to go?* This question often does not have a simple answer; various tools must be employed to answer it in an authentic and effective way. You will need to identify your direction, your strategy, and your vision.

- In the *East*, we ask: *Why do you want to go there?* This question takes you to a deeper level of consideration and can help you avoid any default decision-making pattern that you might have developed. Answering this question well can improve your motivation and verify alignment with your own system of values and drivers.

- In the *West*, we ask: *How will you get there?* What is the step-by-step plan that will allow you to achieve what you really want? How will you execute effective tactics while improving your skills and managing resources? You'll need a good set of skills and tools to help you in planning.

- In the *South*, we ask a question about what is holding you back: *Why not move ahead?* Why are you not doing the things you say you want to do? What stops you? Why delay instead of taking action now? Here you need to detect and overcome barriers and limiting beliefs that prevent you from achieving your goals. This process of gaining self-awareness requires you to identify barriers and break through the boundaries of your comfort zone.

The NEWS™ Model

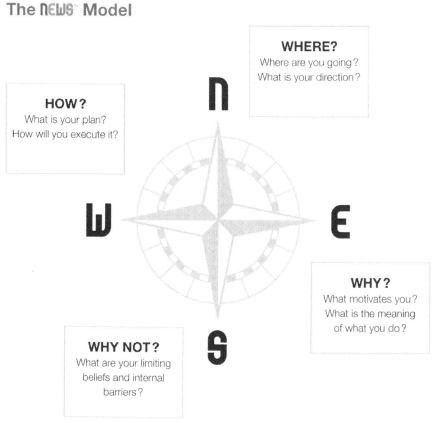

WHERE?
Where are you going?
What is your direction?

HOW?
What is your plan?
How will you execute it?

WHY?
What motivates you?
What is the meaning
of what you do?

WHY NOT?
What are your limiting
beliefs and internal
barriers?

Using the metaphor of the compass, the model associates a particular blockage with each of the four directions.

- In the North, the blockage could be a lack of a clear direction or a vision of the ideal future. This might result in a lack of purpose.

- In the East, the blockage could be the absence of a strong connection to your values, motivations, and drivers. This might result in low energy or motivation, leading to fatigue or burnout.

- In the West, the blockage could be the absence of a plan or the lack of skills or competencies to execute the plan and to reach your objectives. This can result in distraction, lack of focus, and delay in the development and execution of your plan.

- In the South, the blockage could be the presence of inhibitions, fear of failure, or other limiting beliefs that hinder your progress. This often leads to avoidance or procrastination, with many excuses as to why there is no movement or change.

Behind the N.E.W.S. model are ten axioms:

1. Within you, there is a natural potential for greatness.

2. This potential can be manifested in your life, thoughts, and actions—or not.

3. You create your reality by making choices, consciously or unconsciously. Over time, that is how you shape your life.

4. The manifestation of your greatness is a matter of conscious choice.

5. Along the way, you have to overcome internal and external limits and barriers.

6. Overcoming barriers to greatness is a process of learning, growth and development. It requires courage and intelligent risk-taking.

7. Your greatness, your barriers, and therefore your life's journey are individual and particular to you.

8. When you make wise conscious choices, growth occurs at many levels of your being—mental, emotional, and physical.

9. Others can assist you in discovering your potential, your barriers, and the manifestations of your greatness, but they cannot make choices or take your journey for you.

10. Greatness is your inborn and authentic potential; your possible contribution to the world. It's up to you to become that greater self.

Chapter 6

Where Do You Start?

So, where do you start?

I enjoy field navigation (also known as orienteering). My friends and I meet early in the morning and head for someplace far from civilization, carrying backpacks. We navigate for a day or two in terrain that is unfamiliar to us, using only a map and a compass. If you have ever navigated in this way, you probably realized quickly that the first question you needed to answer was not, "Where am I going?" but "Where am I starting from?" The answer is not always simple. We usually tend to look backward ("Where did I come from?") to understand where we are now. But it doesn't always help.

Rick was a brilliant and ambitious young salesperson. He sold phar-maceuticals and always exceeded his sales objectives. On his desk was a plaque that read, "CEO-to-be." When his manager left, Rick was promoted to be the sales team leader. Within two months, two people from the team left, two more looked to leave the company, and sales were down 18 percent. Rick's managerial skills were minimal. He would push his team constantly and abrasively. "Where are the numbers?" he would shout. While his team was falling apart, Rick sat at his desk, looking at his plaque. His true location and situation was no platform for targeting that future.

Before any important endeavor or journey, you need to know where you are starting from. This is a matter of self-awareness—the willingness to be honest with yourself and to look beyond your own perceptions or wishes. Just looking at the trail you are walking on does not give you a full picture of where you are in reality. You need to expand your frame of reference, to "zoom out" from where you are. In field navigation, you look around until you find a hill or a tree or a house, and you then deduce where you are in relation to those elements around you. This is called triangulation: realizing where you are by using at least three external reference points.

To know where you are starting from at a specific time, you need to expand your view; to take an external perspective. You can better understand your position by getting feedback from several different people—a family member, a colleague, a friend, your partner. Although their relationship with you will influence their perceptions, by listening to all of their viewpoints, you can begin to assess your current location more accurately.

You can also look at your situation from different perspectives: mental, emotional, spiritual, physical. You can consider your family situation, your financial condition, and your subjective well-being in order to understand where you are at a particular moment. As in field navigation, when you are navigating your life, you need a number of different reference points to assess where you are.

To better assess your starting point, here is a quick location questionnaire that will indicate to you which of the four directions of the compass you might wish to focus on first. Each set of questions refers to one of the compass directions: North, East, West, or South. In the following section, you will learn about each of these directions in the model and be able to choose where to start and how to proceed, depending on which direction you are interested in pursuing first.

Quick Location Questionnaire[4]

To what degree does each of the following sentences apply to your life at present?

Please score each question and add your scores for each direction.

1: Not at all, 2: Very little, 3: Moderately, 4: A great deal, 5: Completely

North	
1. I have a clear direction for my professional development.	
2. I have established goals for the next five to ten years.	
3. My goals are written down; I use them to guide my choices.	
Total	
Insights and conclusions:	

East	
1. I have a set of values that guides my work.	
2. I apply my values to my work every day.	
3. I am passionate and excited about my work.	
Total	
Insights and conclusions:	

---

4   Reprinted with permission from N.E.W.S.® Coaching and Training. See Resources list for information about a full version of this instrument.

West	
1. I have a clear working plan to achieve my goals.	
2. I have a timeline for achieving my goals.	
3. I plan my time each week guided by my goals.	
Total	
Insights and conclusions:	

South	
1. I focus on personal and professional improvement and development.	
2. I am aware of my barriers and fears and work to overcome them.	
3. I choose to break out of my comfort zone occasionally.	
Total	
Insights and conclusions:	

As you proceed to the next section of the book, find the direction where you think you have the most work to do right now. You will probably want to begin your work in the direction where you believe you are most "stuck"—in other words, where you have given yourself the lowest score. Being stuck means that you need to put your hands on the wheel again. Perhaps you have lost your way at a certain point in your journey; you wander aimlessly or continue to encounter the same obstacles over and over. You feel unable to move on. You may have navigated well in a certain direction in the past, yet find that same direction difficult in your current circumstances. Self-navigation is a lifelong process, sometimes you make small course corrections, sometimes you turn in a new direction.

Begin in the direction that is most challenging for you now and move to another direction when you're ready. There is no right way to do this. Each choice you make will influence other choices. As you navigate toward achieving your vision, you may need to focus at times on your motivation in the East or your barriers in the South or your plans in the West; you may even need to rethink your direction in the North.

Activity

Given the feedback you received from others and the way you have scored yourself on the questionnaire, which direction seems like the right place to start your journey?

Section Two

The Four Directions

Chapter 7

Skills for Self-Navigation

In this section, we will take a deep look at each of the directions, illustrate it with a story, and then discuss in greater detail some of the skills that you will need to be successful as you navigate in that direction. Begin where you believe you are currently "stuck" or perhaps where you feel most ready to move.

There are schools for learning to drive a car or pilot a plane or sail a boat. But opportunities to learn the skills involved in navigating through the choice points in your life are not so obvious. As we discussed earlier, we tend to make decisions by default when we don't bring them to our conscious awareness. In the following chapters, we will explore the four directions and share a set of skills that can be useful to you for understanding, developing, and choosing in each of the quadrants of the compass.

First, let's look at how we learn and develop new competencies. Competencies are generally defined as the skills, knowledge, attitudes, and behaviors required to achieve successful results in a particular task or activity. For practical purposes, we'll use the words *competence* or *competency* and *skill* interchangeably.

Stages in the Development of Competence

There is a natural cycle in the development of competence. The stages of the cycle include the following:

1. **Unawareness**

   You are not conscious of the elements of or the level of competence of your performance.

2. **Dissatisfaction**

   You become aware (through feedback, failure, self-observation, performance pressure, or seeing someone else perform better than you thought possible) that your current level is no longer personally satisfying.

3. **Readiness**

   Once you have absorbed the shock, surprise, disappointment, or excitement of experiencing dissatisfaction (high performers interested in their own growth and development are sometimes thrilled rather than disappointed to see how much more is possible), you can reach a state of readiness for learning or developing skills. This is especially true if you have a vision of what is possible and have the support to achieve it.

4. **Active Learning**

    During this stage, depending on your learning style and preferences, you may observe, watch videos of or interview top performers, research and read articles and books on the topic, practice, attend a seminar, receive coaching, or a combination of these and other approaches.

5. **Performance Awareness**

    As you begin to integrate what you have learned, you experience a heightened awareness of how your performance of the skill is developing. At first, the new or improved skills will feel awkward and unnatural. You may need "crib notes" or self-talk to stay focused on the improved approach so that you avoid returning to your default mode.

6. **Flow**

    Once the new level of skill is fully integrated and you begin to experience success, the new approach is reinforced and eventually becomes part of your repertoire. Instead of feeling awkward, the pattern of behavior has a graceful, smooth flow. At times, this flow is associated with feelings of well-being and delight in the process.

Inevitably, the cycle will continue. At some point, you will once again be unaware that there is a further level of competency. You will need to experience dissatisfaction before reaching that next level.

If possible, it's very useful to involve a coach or a person you trust in your competency development process. This person can observe, provide feedback, and envision what is possible for you. A professional coach or a colleague who acts as a coaching partner can work with you as you learn new approaches and as you improve and adjust. He or she can help you integrate these skills into a strategy for performance and success. Once you have fully integrated the feedback mechanisms and strategies for adjustment and have moved into a state of flow, you have internalized the coach; this internal coach will show up as and when needed.

Active Learning: Developing New Skills

Let's take a closer look at the process of actively learning complex skills. There are three stages in the development of a new skill:

- understanding the concept.

- producing the behavior in isolation.

- integrating the behavior in context.

As you work with a coach or as you guide yourself through developing new skills, make sure these skills are ones that you can actually apply to your own journey. Learning any complex, new skill is something like attending a golf clinic or a tennis camp. You need to understand a skill, practice it in isolation, then integrate into your own approach to the game – or to directing your life.

- Understanding the concept

  To begin, you need to:

  - develop an intellectual understanding of the skill.

  - develop an overview or "big picture" view of how the skill fits into your larger approach, and

  - become familiar with standards for excellence.

- Producing the behavior in isolation

  Once you understand what you are trying to achieve or model, you should:
  - produce the behavior in isolation

  - receive feedback and reflect on your performance, and

  - practice until standards are met or exceeded.

- Integrating the behavior in context

  Now that you can demonstrate the new skill, you will:
  - apply it in more complex and realistic practice sessions

  - combine it with related skills, and

  - integrate it into real situations.

You have probably already identified some areas where you wish to develop new or improved skills. In this section of the book, you will learn some specific ways in which you can become more competent as a navigator of your life.

Chapter 8

The North

The North symbolizes the North Star or the North magnetic pole. These have been the main tools of navigation since ancient times. They are always there; they are easy to find and to navigate by. Likewise, in our model, the North has to do with targeting, with tuning your intention and focusing it—with using it as a driving force. The North deals with direction, strategy, and vision. As you approach any choice point, crossroad, or major decision, the first questions that come to mind are "Where do I want to go?" "What is my destination?" "What results do I want to achieve?"

The work to be done in the North is systematic; step by step. When things are complex, working on the North delivers what Oliver Wendell Holmes Jr. called "the simplicity on the other side of complexity." This work is like wielding the sword that cuts through the Gordian knot. A Phrygian legend tells of Alexander the Great being confronted with this complex knot, which an oracle suggested could predict the next ruler of Asia. When he could not find the end of the knot to unbind it, he sliced it in half with a stroke of his sword. This story is often used as a metaphor for solving a complex and difficult problem in an unexpected or creative way.

Knowing where you intend to go provides clarity, engenders hope, and creates energy and a sense of momentum. The question of where you see yourself heading is not an easy one. You may find it difficult to address, especially if you have just lost a job or completed a project, or if you face a major life or career decision. You may, at times, find yourself "stuck in the North" without a clear sense of a direction to navigate toward.

The words *vision, mission, goals, direction, objective,* and *strategy* are all associated with movement toward a desired state. These words are used differently by different people and organizations. Here is a glossary to clarify how we are using these terms in this book:

Terms Associated with the Future

- *Direction*: the broad area in which you wish to progress

- *Mission:* your authentic calling within that direction

- *Vision:* your image of a desired future reality

- *Strategy:* a "practical model" for the next step in your direction

- *Goals:* purposeful and specific results on the way to achieving your vision

- *Objectives:* defined and measurable milestones toward achieving each goal

Some people believe that looking toward the North should start with defining a vision. Over the years, we have found that, for many people, a vision is a set of words that hangs on a conference room wall or appears in an annual report to stockholders. For others, it is a fantasy that they have about the future—an escape from current circumstances rather than something they truly believe in and desire.

A forty-two-year-old friend once said that his "vision" was to retire and relax in a hammock between two coconut trees in the Caribbean. When I asked him why, he replied that he was so tired and burnt out from work that this was the only "vision" he could have. I asked how long he thought he could sustain that life. He had no clear answer; the vision was more a reaction to the present than a desire for the future. Another friend's vision was to become the CEO of his company. When asked why, he replied, "Everyone wants to climb the corporate ladder. Why shouldn't I?"

When achieved, these shortsighted visions often leave a person unsatisfied and unfulfilled. The N.E.W.S.™ model is meant to help people create a compelling vision that is deeply connected to them, to their real passions and capabilities. When people achieve such a vision, they feel authentically fulfilled and satisfied. This is why we start in the North by exploring the best and most fulfilling direction for you at a specific time in your life.

Your Direction

Direction is the broad area in which you would like to make progress. How do people choose their direction? Some choose according to what we call a survival or mediocrity model. They ask themselves questions like these: How can I take less risk? How can I play it safe? Where do they pay reasonable wages? What am I not too bad at doing? What can I do with minimal effort? This kind of thought pattern usually leads people to choose a direction of study, work, and engagement that will not be motivating and will not create real and sustainable value for them or for others. This approach leads to mediocrity, boredom, and lack of fulfillment.

Others might choose a direction based on what others (family, teachers, society) think or expect, even if it is not a compelling and inspiring direction to them. For example, your father is a lawyer, so you apply to law school. People of your gender are supposed to be bad at math, so you avoid pursuing a career in science or engineering. Your spouse has a high need for security, so you stay with a safe but boring corporate job rather than striking out on your own as an entrepreneur.

We suggest, instead, that you choose your next direction according to the Greatness model. This model, researched and applied over many years and with many individuals, allows people to have greater self-fulfillment and better motivation, and to make more valuable contributions. According to this model, when defining a direction, you need to ask yourself questions like these:

- What am I passionate about?

- What are my talents and core competencies?

- What was I born to do?

- What could I do that would make me happy and excited to get to work every day?

Some people may find these questions difficult to answer. Maybe they have lost their authentic passions; they cannot recall what excites them anymore. Should you find yourself in that situation, think back to an earlier time in your life when you were enjoying the present and excited about the future. The clues lie there—in your genuine pleasure in doing what is fulfilling, exciting, even fun.

Next, look at where your responses intersect with one another. You will want to choose a direction that you are both passionate about and have the capability to achieve. This is your "direction of greatness," your potential contribution to the world. You can then write a sentence that expresses this intersection clearly. You might want to work with a friend or a coach to help you identify the right way to describe this direction. Here are some direction sentences we have heard:

- "To coach people to become outstanding leaders."

- "To manufacture healthy food for children."

- "To produce inspiring cultural events."

- "To provide world-class hospitality."

- "To create a management system that makes order out of chaos."

- "To lead individuals and organizations to breakthroughs."

Practical Model

Once you have a direction sentence, it's time to think about a practical model, or strategy for moving in that direction. In ancient Greek, a *strategos* was the leader of an army. He was called that because he had to have an overview of the whole plane, or *strata* in Greek, of the battle. He had to stand on a hill behind the army, where he could view the entire battlefield. Strategy is the ability to make major decisions and to maneuver, having seen the overall picture.

Your practical model is a structure or arrangement that will allow you to operate within your direction in a realistic way. It needs to be authentic to you (expressing your direction sentence), realistic, financially viable, and a good fit for your circumstances. Choosing your best practical model could be a matter of research or of innovation.

The practical model might exist already—perhaps it is the role that you currently hold, but with a change of emphasis or a remix of activities. Perhaps another role in your organization better expresses your direction. It could be an opportunity that already exists outside of your current situation. For example, you might join an existing partnership or register for an academic program. For some people, however, discovering their true North might mean a radical change, such as moving or changing their lifestyle and economic expectations.

Perhaps a practical model does not exist, and you need to innovate. You might develop a type of service or product that no one yet provides, a role that does not yet exist in your company, or a new business model. Whether you find your model within an existing situation or create something new, your solution needs to be feasible. It should fit your current needs and support the kind of life you wish to have. Your practical model may simply involve optimizing your present situation.

Rebecca was an accountant, and her direction sentence was about helping people in need. She created a practical solution: she would work in her accountant role four days a week and one day a week she would volunteer in a special project that taught algebra to children from poor neighborhoods.

George was a high-school business teacher, but really wanted to be a leadership coach. His direction was to coach people to high performance. His practical model was to create a coaching practice for owners of small to medium business in addition to his teaching position. Later, when he had eight regular clients, he resigned from his teaching job and devoted himself to coaching.

We call this type of practical solution "repositioning," whereby a person builds the next boat while sailing in the existing one. When the new boat is ready, according to predetermined indicators, the person can jump from the old boat to the new one. This model eliminates much of the stress and fear that comes with taking bold and risky actions early on.

Vision

Vision, as we use the term, is a practical tool. It is a detailed, tangible picture of the future you want to create. Ask yourself, "If I put my practical model to work, what would be the best case scenario in two to three years?" Your vision needs to be practical, attainable, concrete, detailed, and of a magnitude that you can aspire to.

When you have such a vision, it is like having a lighthouse you can sail toward. A well-designed vision provides energy, hope, and the drive to get there. You might have a vision of the business you will create, the place you will live, or the type of life you will lead.

I learned a great deal about the power of vision from my friend, Illit. She was a happy, lively woman in her thirties, running a successful production company with her husband. They had two beautiful children. Illit was living exactly the kind of life she had always wanted. One day she was diagnosed with breast cancer. Her world collapsed. She was told that she would have to undergo a long series of difficult treatments, but that she could survive.

On the day before the treatments started, she made a few important decisions: first, she would recover; second, she would document her recovery in a film; and third, she would write a book about her recovery as a guide for other breast cancer patients. She also decided that when she recovered, she would have a great celebration to thank all of those who supported her.

Illit then went through the most difficult two years of her life. She told me that in her darkest moments, when she felt like dying, she would imagine the thank-you party. She thought of the kind of music she would play, the dress and shoes she would wear, the dancing. "That is what kept me going in those moments," she told everyone at the amazing thank-you party I was privileged to attend.

Such is the power of a real and practical vision. It can carry you beyond great difficulties. As Nietzsche said, "When you have a strong enough *why*, you can bear almost any *how*." We do know

now, through scientific studies, that when you imagine images of the future, your brain produces neuropeptides that create a delight sensation, as if you had already achieved it. A vision is necessary for greatness, though not sufficient. Research also shows, perhaps counter-intuitively, that if you *only* create a vision and don't consider possible obstacles and how you will overcome them, you are less likely to succeed than people without a vision.

Why do so many people fail to have a vision that will carry them through adversity? I believe that many of them are not aware of the power of envisioning possibilities. They are afraid to have great visions, because this increases the stakes and makes failure more disappointing. Michelangelo said, "The problem of most people is not that they aim too high and fail. The problem with most people is that they aim too low and succeed." Vision requires an active imagination. As children, we are all able to imagine, but as formal education and the experiences of life take their toll, many find it more and more difficult to create a positive picture of the future in their mind's eye.

Questions

1. When you think about the future, what positive, energizing pictures come to your mind?

2. What do you dream of achieving? When you were young, what were your dreams?

Kirsten

Kirsten Swenson is forty-seven years old. She has been an entrepreneur for ten years. Her business, a high-end linen shop featuring beautiful imported items, has flourished even through difficult economic times. She has had several offers to buy it, which she has always refused. Recently, however, she has begun feeling weary of the twelve-hour days and the lack of time for herself and her family. Kirsten is a single mother of twin boys, now juniors in high school. She has managed to be involved with their activities—sports teams, debate team, drama club performances— but has seldom had time to sit and have quiet conversations with them. Between her business and her children, there is no time or energy left for seeing friends or developing her own interests.

She would like more balance in her life. Should she sell the company and start something new? Should she go to work for someone else? Should she get someone to manage her business? Should she take a sabbatical and then decide? She feels that she could use some help; her thoughts are not resolving in any particular direction, and she is getting tired of being locked into this situation.

Kirsten decides to work with a coach. During their first meeting, she comes to the realization that it has been many years since she asked herself important questions about what she loves to do and is good at doing. The two of them spend considerable time pursuing these questions. After some discussion, she realizes that she has been so focused on raising her children, making a living, and creating a successful business that she has lost sight of her early passion for art. She had attended art school nearly every Saturday of her life from the age of seven until she was fourteen. She had enjoyed drawing, painting, pottery, and sculpture. But when it came time to choose a career, she followed in her father's footsteps and completed a degree in business, then worked in retail environments very successfully before opening her store.

"I think it's too late for me to consider a career in the arts," Kirsten tells her coach, Jude. "The only thing I do that is even vaguely related to art is photographing my children and their friends as they practice for a game or rehearse for a play." Kirsten smiles a little as she says this and holds out her smartphone to show Jude some examples of her photos.

"These are really interesting," Jude says. "I see that you have a keen eye for composition."

"Do you think so? I have always loved arranging things in my store, maybe that's been my way of expressing my inner artist. I wish I had more time to work on my photography; I'd love to learn more about the technical side of it. I certainly have the passion for it, and it seems that I could be quite good at this."

Kirsten leaves the coaching session with a lot to think about. How could she find a direction that would allow her to let her inner artist out more often? What might be a practical model for her? What would she be able to do that would provide an income that would support two boys in college?

At the next meeting, Kirsten surprises Jude with the news that she has found her direction and a strategy—what Jude calls a practical model. "I know how to run a successful shop," she says. "I believe that I could learn to run a successful art gallery. That could be my direction. I would like to have a gallery that specializes in work by up-and-coming photographers. This would mean becoming part of a community of people with something to teach me that I want to learn about, while still using the skills that have made me successful so far. Arranging the shows would give me a lot of satisfaction, and perhaps at some point I could even have a show of my own work."

"Is that practical?" Jude asks.

"Oh, yes. There is a great deal of interest in art photography in this town and no galleries that specialize in that kind of work."

While Kirsten believes she has found her true North and practical model, she knows that she has a lot of work to do in making new network connections, learning about a new kind of business, studying photography, selling her old business, contracting with the right artists, and planning for and opening her gallery.

"My vision for eighteen months from now," Kirsten can now say with ambition, clarity, and enthusiasm, "is to have the grand opening of my photography gallery with a show that gets great critical reviews, gives a leg up to some young and talented artists, provides me a decent living, and at least breaks even financially."

Skills for the North

When your compass is pointing to the North, your work is about finding your direction, identifying a practical model for achieving it, and creating a vision of success. Just as Kirsten did, you will need to think strategically. This includes

- framing and reframing the issue,

- identifying opportunities, and

- crafting a vision.

Kirsten wanted to do something that would use her existing talents and provide for her family. To move forward, she first needed to clarify her direction. Like Kirsten, use your ability to frame problems, issues, and opportunities in multiple ways to help identify a general direction that is right for you.

Framing and Reframing

Framing is the structure and meaning that you give to a set of data. You construct a container for the observable facts. For example, you notice a colleague at his desk with his head in his hands. You create meaning out of the situation by assuming that he has just heard some bad news. This gives you an idea of how to respond to him. But then you remember that he sometimes suffers from cluster headaches. If that is what is going on, you would respond differently. In constructing a meaningful frame for any situation, you add your own interpretation of what the facts indicate. The frame you give something both defines and limits the way you see it and the way you respond to it. When framing, you are adding certain interpretations and possible solutions and removing others. The way you frame an issue is a limiting factor in how you think about and approach it. Therefore, it is often useful to frame an issue or problem in a number of different ways and then, using your own criteria, select the most effective frame to use. *Effective* means the one that will provide the best possible results for you. That could mean the broadest one, the most neutral one, or the one that is most challenging for you.

Being flexible in the way you frame things requires you to consider the possibility that there is no one right answer or solution. You have to develop the ability to live with ambiguity and to appreciate the freedom involved in expanding your options. Kirsten worked through multiple ways of framing her issue and her direction.

- "I want a less taxing job."

- "I want to find a way to help other people."

- "I want to find a way to use my sales skills to help others be successful."

- "I want to use my entrepreneurial skills to help artists to succeed."

Each different way she framed her direction meant framing some possibilities in while ignoring others.

Once you have framed an issue, it may be difficult to see it any other way. The classic optical illusions take advantage of this human tendency. Is it an old woman or a young belle? Is the box concave or convex? You have to train yourself to see something in a new way, and each time you expand the options, you break through a fixed perception into a new possibility. The good news is that once you have done this a few times, you are fully aware that there are multiple ways of seeing a picture, an issue, or a potential direction, even if you are able to see only one at a time.

Kirsten wasn't satisfied with the first frame (a less taxing job); it limited her options and required that she depend on others to offer something that fit her frame. As she considered the facts of the situation, she realized that she was most enthusiastic about aspects of her work that involved helping others to succeed. Eventually she landed on a direction statement that met her near-term needs and allowed her to create a practical model and to envision a future where she could live out her dream. Kirsten's experience illustrates the importance of taking care that we don't lock in on the first or most obvious frame or the one that is easiest to consider.

Chris Argyris developed the idea of a "ladder of inference"[5]—a way to move from how you currently frame an issue down through several layers of assumptions and interpretations until you reach the basic set of data that is at the bottom of the ladder. The skill of reframing involves climbing down that ladder and then arranging the objectively or historically observable data you find there in a number of different ways without going through the usual step of deciding quickly on a "correct" interpretation. You develop several possible frames and

---

5   Described in Peter Senge, et al., *The Fifth Discipline Fieldbook: Strategies and Tools for Building a Learning Organization* (New York: Crown Business, 1994).

then consider each one as a source of ideas, solutions, or directions, aware that different frames will lead you toward different possibilities.

The information Kirsten found at the bottom of her "ladder of inference" (the basic set of data that she had started from) included the following:

- She needed an income.

- She needed to have a more balanced life.

- She had been successful as an entrepreneur.

- She enjoyed working with customers.

- She enjoyed and was successful at nurturing younger people.

- She was interested in art.

- She was a talented photographer.

- She had a lot of experience in retail business.

Her original direction (finding a less taxing job) was framed based on only the first two pieces of information. As she thought more about her work history and her own passions and talents, she broadened her frames to include many other possibilities. These could be arranged in many different ways. Eventually she narrowed the frame to what she saw as the most promising way to create a direction for her career.

Another approach to framing and reframing is to begin by defining a challenge. A good way to define a challenge is to look at the desired result you hope to achieve. Using a phrase like "Wouldn't it be great if..." you can express the ideal outcome. For example, Kirsten defined her challenge in this way: "Wouldn't it be great if I could make money doing something I love to do." You can write several challenges, then select one and frame it as an issue.

Try framing the issue in three different ways. A good frame should include the result you are aiming for in broad terms. Kirsten might have framed her issue in any of the following ways:

- To find a job I love

- To find a type of business where I can learn while I earn

- To create an opportunity to make money while doing something I love to do.

The third frame opened up broader possibilities for Kirsten.

Identifying Opportunities

As we discussed earlier, a strategic approach to achieving success in the direction you have chosen is to design a practical model for approaching it. What opportunities will allow you to actualize your direction? Thinking this through requires careful monitoring of five basic factors of any strategic opportunity or practical model: the *who*, the *why*, the *what*, the *how*, and the *where*.

*1. **Who** am I? What am I passionate about and good at?*
When have you felt the most happy and fulfilled in your work or personal life? What have others said to you about what you were "born to do"? What does this tell you about your natural preferences and talents?

*2. **Why** do I need to move in a new direction?*
Here you will visit your East to uncover your core values and drivers as well as considering external factors such as a change in your job status or a move.

*3. **What** should I focus on?*
Here you will consider how much further you can go with what you already know how to do and ask yourself what you are drawn to that would be new for you and expand your possibilities.

*4.   **How** can I make a clear move in this direction?*
At this point, you will consider how ready you are to make this move and develop a number of alternative models for doing it, given your state of readiness. Here you will ask yourself questions, such as:

- What would it take for me to be ready to make a move, no matter how small, in this new direction? What would have to change? How willing am I to make that change?

- What alternatives exist as ways for me to begin my move in this direction?

*5. **Where** is there a market for what I want to do?*
Now you will consider questions such as these:

- What needs exist that I could fulfill?

- What could I do that would meet those needs while simultaneously moving me along in the direction that I want to go?

- How could I create a need among people or organizations that don't yet recognize the possibilities of what I could offer? How can these alternatives become viable economically?

The last questions invite you to observe others from an ethnographic point of view, as if you were an anthropologist studying another culture. People and organizations don't know what they don't know. For example, ten or fifteen years ago, few of us thought we would need a phone that could keep track of our appointments, entertain us with music and games, and allow us to communicate with our friends and colleagues in multiple ways.

Kirsten's breakthrough came when she could see that there were opportunities for her to use her previous success pattern as an entrepreneur in a different context. The skill of identifying opportunities flows from your ability to be true to yourself and your direction while being flexible about how that direction can be expressed and acted on.

Crafting a Vision

Once you have identified your direction and practical model, you are ready to create a vision of success—picturing the ideal result of pursuing such a strategy by a specific time. Envisioning is a process of determining where you want to go and how you will know that you have arrived. A clear vision sustains motivation even at difficult times and enables you to communicate with stakeholders, sponsors, and resource people, and to influence them to join or support you.

The kind of vision we are talking about is not a terse statement that appears on corporate coffee cups and annual reports. Instead, we mean a way of projecting yourself—and sometimes others—into a desired future that could occur if you succeed with your practical model. This vision will be your North Star—something you can use to steer by. The language will be rich and sensory. Your vision will draw you continuously toward its fulfillment.

An effective vision meets the following criteria:

- Positive

- Optimistic—possible, but requires a stretch

- Focused on ends, not means

- Aligned with important goals and values

- Expressed in engaging, sensory language

- Inspiring and motivating to you.

As you develop your vision, consider the following questions:

- What will I see, hear, sense, or experience that is different from the way things are now?

- Who will benefit from this positive result? In what ways?

- How will I and my stakeholders and supporters feel about the result?

One way to make your vision seem more real and engaging is to use the present tense to describe it—as if it has already happened. Kirsten's vision begins like this: "It's the opening night of my first gallery show. I'm welcoming guests who are potential customers as well as the artists whose photographs hang on the walls. The space is designed to be warm and inviting; my guests are fascinated by the new work."

Of course, your vision will change as you navigate and achieve success—or perhaps as you need to shift your direction due to unexpected winds of change.

Activities

1. Begin with a draft direction statement, one that answers the questions "Where do I want to go?" and "What direction should I take?" At this point, you may want to move to your East to explore your drivers—your values, needs, and motivations.

2. Use the draft statement to frame three to five different possible directions. Begin each one with the word *to*.

3. Answer the following questions to help you create a practical model:

   - Who am I, at the deepest level? What am I passionate about, and what was I "born to do"?

   - Why do I need to change the direction of my life? And why now?

   - What should I take as my main area of focus? To what degree can I apply what I am already skillful at, and what do I need to learn?

   - How can I begin my journey in the new direction? How big or how small should my first move be?

   - Where are opportunities for me to create value and receive the satisfaction of making a unique contribution?

4. If you put your practical model to work, what might be a best-case scenario (vision) for you three years from now? Write a two- or three-sentence paragraph describing in

detail what success would look like. Create an engaging vision of success with your practical model. Describe in rich, sensory terms what that success would look like, sound like, feel like. Project yourself into a future when that success has been achieved, and write your vision in the present tense, describing what *is* rather than what might be. Ask yourself these questions:

- What will I have achieved?

- What has the impact been on others?

- How do I and others feel about it?

5. Test your vision against the criteria suggested earlier in this chapter. Read it aloud and explain it to someone you trust; then ask for feedback on how enthusiastic and how committed you seem.

Chapter 9

The East

If the North is where you are sailing, the East is the wind that blows your sails and moves you in the right direction. From the East come your deeper motivations, your energy and passion, your inner voice. An old Latin saying is "From the East comes the light; from the West comes the law." The Romans observed that the sun comes from the east, and many Eastern cultures focus on enlightenment and internal motivation.

The East in our navigation model has to do with our authentic values, our internal drivers, our deepest motivations. When you identify and connect to it, the East is like an engine that takes you past obstacles and allows you to achieve your most desired results. The East is often in dialogue with the South. At any choice point, the East suggests why you should pay attention to your intuition or inner voice, while the South whispers in your ear why you should not—listing all the risks you'll be taking if you follow your heart.

Being stuck in the East means you have lost touch with your internal motivations; you feel burned out; you lack energy. Your plane's engine has stopped working, and you are losing speed and altitude. These moments occur when we are not fully connected and engaged with our work or with other aspects of our life. External motivations such as money, status, and power may not be enough to sustain our interest and engagement in either our work or our personal life for very long. Responding to our deep internal motivations brings passion, intensity, determination, and joy to our lives. We call the most important of these our "core" motivators.

Core Motivators

There are three steps involved in exploring the East. The first is to discover what is driving and motivating you now; the second is to connect to these motivators in an authentic way; and the third is to translate those drivers into your direction (North) and into your behaviors and actions (West).

The process of discovery in the East is stimulated by the question "Why?" Why do you want to go in that direction? What is important for you about it? What is "core" where you are concerned?

I remember a session I once led with senior leaders of a bank. One of them was a customer service manager who was seen by her colleagues as bitter and aggressive. They had known her for many years and were careful not to upset her in any way. Thinking it odd that she was in a customer contact role, I asked her in the open forum of the group why she had chosen that particular position. She replied that it had happened many years before.

"But why did you choose it?" I asked.

"The position was vacant, so I chose it," she replied, frowning.

I continued to prod. "But why you? And why customer service?"

After giving a few curt responses to my continuing "why" questions, she finally shouted, "Because I love to work with people!"

Everyone was surprised, including her. It was the first time in thirty years that she remembered why she had chosen what she had been doing all that time. She obviously had become disassociated from her original motivation; a drive to relate to and serve other people. She was not connected to it, nor did she translate it into her behavior during the many years she worked in that role.

The more deeply you probe with questions like "Why do you do what you do?" or "Why do you want to choose that direction or vision?" the more specific and profound the answers will be. The Socratic Method suggests that if you ask "Why?" enough times, you will get closer to the whole truth. (Eventually, Socrates was made to drink poison—not everyone likes to be exposed to the truth.)

To identify what moves you authentically, explore what is currently most important to you, and then break it down to its constituent elements. If you say that people are important, ask why that is. What is important about people for you? If you answer, "Communication," you can then ask, "What is it about communication?" If your answer to that is "To transfer ideas," you can ask, "What is important to you about that?" Eventually, you might discover that the core driver for you is the ability to create something important, together with others.

Another way to come at this is to think about how you want to be remembered. How would you want your work or relationships to be summarized in the future? This kind of questioning might surface what is most important and help you identify the key elements that drive you.

This is a deep process. If you come back to it at different times in your life, you might discover that your answers become richer and more refined. In your East, you may discover the essence of your being or the core elements of your authentic motivation.

Personal Values

The key words or phrases that you identify as important internal drivers will be a summary of your core values—such as *creativity, respect, freedom of choice*. If you get all the way to recognizing the constituent elements, you will know what makes you tick, what gets you up in the morning, and what makes your eyes shine. You will understand the basis of your important life decisions—or what can be the basis for them in the future.

Values are related to norms, but are more global and abstract. Norms are rules for behavior in specific situations. Values specify what you believe to be intrinsically important, good, right, or desirable; they guide your judgment and behavior. Your core values shape your decisions and priorities. The relative importance of certain values may change over time, but once you have reached a certain level of maturity, your core values are relatively stable. At different times, depending on what is at stake, different core values may be the major drivers in your decisions.

Rank and test these values. According to Sidney Simon,[6] values that are not actively used to make decisions and guide behavior are

6   Sidney Simon, Leland Howe, and Howard Kirschenbaum, *Values Clarification,* (New York: Grand Central Publishing, 1995).

aspirations rather than values—something you *aspire* to use to drive your behavior and decisions. They can become values, but only if they are allowed to drive your actions. It's also vital to understand the order of importance among our values. If a situation occurs and you have conflicting values in relation to it, you know where to place the most emphasis and importance. In the next section, we will suggest some activities that will help you to define and clarify your core values.

Once you have tested and ranked your values, you can consciously connect deeply to them. People who are conscious and connected to their core values navigate themselves more easily in the sea of uncertainty. They feel much more confident as to what they stand for. They know what they will agree to as well as what they will say no to, even when a new opportunity is tempting. When you are clear on your core values, your foundation is solid and you can be confident in decision making.

When we explore our values deeply, we discover who we are— what makes us unique. Each of us has a particular mix of three or four core values that do not really change; they are like the DNA of our motivation. At different times in life, different values become the most important drivers, and the whole navigation system has to be aligned accordingly.

Once you are well connected to your East, it is time to translate it so it becomes the driving force of your endeavor. The East can be translated into your North (practical model) or into your West (behavior). Your deep motivations will affect your practical model. For example, if family life is a core value for you, you might take a part-time job or work from home for a while. Or perhaps you value exploration, learning, and freedom. To express these, you might create a practical model that involves traveling and meeting new and interesting people.

The East can also be translated into your activities and behaviors in the West. In this case, you will act according to your chosen values. When your behavior does not match your values, there is a gap for you to close. We call it the "be—do gap." It is the space between who you want to be and how you express yourself through your actions. This is likely to be most noticeable in challenging circumstances or with challenging people.

Deeply held values that are authentic to you will manifest themselves in many areas of your life as they radiate from your core. For example, if you value harmony with other people, this will be reflected in your behavior in conflict situations. "Harmony with other people" will affect your behavior at work, in your family, and in your community. This is one way to know that something is a core value for you and not just an aspiration or a habit.

Questions

1. Thinking about times you have enjoyed your work or leisure activities the most, why were they enjoyable, exciting, or motivating?

2. What would a great day at work look like? Sound like? Feel like? What would make it so meaningful, satisfying or stimulating?

3. What values would you stand up for, even fight to defend?

Anna

Anna Chen is in her early fifties. Her background is in sales and marketing, where she was quite successful for a number of years as a medical representative in a large pharmaceutical company, working with physicians. She became a supervisor and really enjoyed helping with the development of new reps just out of college.

Anna took a few years off to focus on her family while her husband supported them, but now her youngest child has entered college, and her husband's business is not flourishing. Anna is feeling bored and restless. She needs to find her way back into the workforce for both financial and personal reasons. She is now asking herself whether she should take a sales job that pays well, regardless of whether it seems like a good fit for her interests.

She knows that she will not be able to get anything like her previous position at her age. She definitely does not want to go to work for one small firm she has heard from, as they can offer only commissions, not a salary. Things are getting more difficult financially for her family; their savings are running out.

Anna thinks that perhaps she should consider starting her own business as a consultant in sales and marketing. She decides to invest in a seminar that a friend has recommended. If she can come away from it with a plan, it will be worth her investment of time and money.

During the seminar, Anna learns that she has followed her North direction well in previous jobs. She develops a new direction sentence for herself. It is "to help others become successful salespeople." Her practical model is "to provide consulting services to small businesses in order to help them to improve their sales and increase their revenue."

Working with a partner during the seminar, she begins to explore the East: the values and motivations that drive her and create personal meaning from the work she does. Sabina, a former colleague and her partner in the exercise, asks her to identify her most important values.

"I'd have to say that, at least where work is concerned, they are authenticity, helping others succeed, and friendship," Anna says.

"That explains to me why you were such a successful salesperson when we worked together," replies Sabina. "All of the docs thought you were their best friend. But I wonder why your direction has shifted toward consulting rather than direct sales?"

"I want to do more than I could on my own. It was enough in the old days for me to make a lot of money on commissions and be recognized for my great sales skills. Now I feel as if I could create greater value by helping others succeed. I was thinking about how I might support small, local businesses in their marketing and sales. I believe I could connect better to my values and express them when doing this type of work. I guess that contributing to my community is an important value for me as well. So I feel excited about this. If I could work this out, I know I'd be putting my heart into it, and the people I work with will get great value out of it. I'm sure I will be satisfied as well by making a real difference."

"So, in the words of the old Tom Lehrer song that you used to sing at work, you want to be 'doing well by doing good.'"

"The 'doing well' part might be difficult. I'll have to figure out if I can make enough money this way."

Sabina has an idea. "I know of an institute that works with freelance consultants who help small businesses in the Bay Area. It's funded by a local foundation. They're looking for more consultants right now. Maybe I could connect you with them."

Anna's face lights up. "Great! I'll call you right after the workshop. I'm ready to get started."

Skills for the East

When you deal with the East, you become aware of your core motivators and values. Skills that are useful in this quadrant include:

- defining and clarifying values

- self-observation, and

- understanding motivation.

Defining and Clarifying Values

Values are the set of principles or beliefs that we regard as right and true. We esteem them highly, and they drive our decision making. They are usually formed early in life, based on our culture, our family, and the people and experiences we are exposed to when we are young. At first, we usually accept them as given, but as we grow and develop, we may test and question them. Different people have a natural affinity to different value sets. The process of discovering your most deeply held values and how they affect your motivations and decision-making is called "values clarification." Once somewhat controversial because it caused young people to question traditional values, this methodology, developed by Sidney Simon, PhD,[7] and others, enables adults to assess, explore, and recommit to core values and to understand how they affect personal choices.

---

7   Sidney Simon, Leland Howe, and Howard Kirschenbaum, *Values Clarification* (New York: Grand Central Publishing, 1995).

The first step in understanding and clarifying your values is to distinguish among three concepts: facts, assumptions, and values. Facts are data—objective evidence that something is true. Assumptions are the meaning we make from observing a selected set of data. Values are the beliefs we hold, based on those assumptions, about what is right and wrong. For example, three people are sitting at a table in the company cafeteria, each looking at a mobile device (fact). You infer that they all work for the company and must know one another (assumption). You think: *They should be talking to one another rather than being in isolated "bubbles."* You have made a judgment and formed an opinion based on your belief that communication among colleagues is important (value).

Sometimes what we call a value is no more than a lofty aspiration. We think it is a good thing and would like to have others see us as holding this value. However, we don't act on it nor are we willing to pay the price for speaking up about it in politically difficult situations. People generally say that they value honesty, for example, but research shows that most people are willing to cheat—just a little—if they believe that they won't be caught. There were many white people in the American South who disapproved of segregation and said—among themselves—that they valued equality, but the social stigma of being an integrationist (there were worse names) kept them from speaking up to neighbors who disagreed.

Some values are widely held within and across societies; others are attached to certain families, groups, professions, and organizations. We were all exposed to cultural, family, professional, and organizational values early in our lives or careers. Some of these we accepted without question; some we had a natural affinity for; others we tested and reconsidered as we matured in our lives or professions. Certain other values are products of our life experience; we choose and act on them based on what we have learned to believe is right and important.

In this chapter, we'll focus on the values that are deep and personal, those that lead you to choose one path over another, one action, rather than another. When your decisions are consistent with your deeply held values, those choices feel right. But you may be operating on values that you inherited or accepted as part of your culture, profession, or organization that simply don't move you as they once did or no longer feel right. Our values can and do change and deepen as we grow.

In Anna's discussion with Sabina, she discovers that just making money for its own sake or achieving recognition for her skills no longer motivated her as they did when she was younger. Her values are more community-oriented now.

Louis Raths, Merrill Harmon, and Sidney Simon[8] developed a set of criteria for determining core personal values. Core values are

- chosen freely rather than enforced by an authority

- selected from among alternatives (we recognize that there are options and choose the one that seems right to us after thoughtful consideration)

- owned (we are willing to stand up and be counted, to affirm the value publicly

- used consistently (we apply the value to important decisions in all aspects of our life).

---

8   Louis Raths, Merrill Harmon, and Sidney B. Simon, *Values and Teaching* (Columbus: C. E. Merrill Books, 1966).

The value-definition process begins by trying to understand what a specific value means to you. What does it relate to? What are the words that you associate with it? Where do you see it in action? When you are satisfied with the content that you attributed to that value or driver, it is time to connect to it in another way. You might want to create a symbol or think about an analogy or metaphor that summarizes it. These right-brained tools will connect you to your core values and drivers in a more emotional or sensory way.

Very often, people have an intuition or deep feeling about the words they choose to describe their values. However, when you ask them what they actually mean by those words, they find it difficult to define them. In trying to connect more deeply with your core values, it's important to define the words using the meaning that you personally attribute to them. Most of us are not trained to define our values; it can be a challenging process. Here are some examples of definitions from participants in our workshops:

- Respect: "The quality of attributing value to other people and their ideas."

- Care: "The ability to anticipate others' needs."

- Integrity: "Being fully integrated around one's principles."

- Support: "Extending active assistance to others."

- Success: "Achieving your desired results."

One way to define and clarify your own values is to think about times when you made important decisions in a conscious way. What criteria did you apply to those decisions? List those criteria, and then rank them in order of importance for you today. For example, Anna listed the following values as criteria she has used for making decisions over the past twenty years:

- Being a good parent

- Being the best at my work

- Helping others to grow and develop

- Being a good friend

- Being ethical in my actions

- Supporting my family well

- Contributing to my community.

She found that some of them were consistent over time, and some of them changed in their importance or in the way they were expressed. For example, her value for being a good mother moved her to work from home and for less time while her children were going through a difficult period. Now that they were launched, she felt that she could be a good mother while working full time. She found that her value for contributing to the community had become more important. This reoriented her toward a new direction.

Self-Observation

"Know thyself" is a popular maxim attributed to various ancient Greek philosophers; it was quoted as common wisdom by Plato, among many others. Modern behavioral science research suggests that, while we believe that we know ourselves well, our confidence is not well placed. For example, we consistently judge our driving ability to be superior to that of others and better than it actually is. We generally attribute positive motives to our own behavior, while being more skeptical of the motives of others. Our decision-making processes, which we believe to be open and rational, are frequently biased by the way a question is framed or by who framed the choice for us.

Introspection can be an indirect, unreliable process of inference. Malcolm Gladwell[9] noted many instances when people were able to accomplish mental tasks quickly, but could not explain how they did so. Recent work in behavioral economics by authors such as Daniel Kahneman, Richard Thaler, and Dan Ariely demonstrates that our decisions are frequently made unconsciously, based on external influences of which we are unaware. Knowing ourselves is not as simple a matter as it might seem.

---

9 Malcolm Gladwell, *Blink: The Power of Thinking Without Thinking* (New York: Little, Brown, 2005).

Johari Window

	Known to self	Not know to self
Known to others		
	Arena	Blind spot
Not known to others		
	Façade	Unknown

The Johari Window,[10] though its name sounds exotic, was actually created by two American university professors, Joseph Luft and Harry Ingham. The model suggests that the traits, characteristics, and motivations of each person can be sorted into four categories or aspects: those that are known to both self and others, those that can be seen by others but not by the self, those that are known by the self but not known to others, and those that are entirely unknown. The "arena"—the area known both to self and others—can be enlarged through self-disclosure (letting more be known by others) or by asking for and receiving feedback (learning how others see oneself). The "blind spot" can be reduced by asking for and listening to feedback from others. The "unknown" area can be explored and minimized through experimenting and taking risks as well as by undertaking certain therapeutic processes and through self-observation.

---

10 J. Luft and H. Ingham, "The Johari Window, a Graphic Model Of Interpersonal Awareness." *Proceedings of the Western Training Laboratory in Group Development* (Los Angeles: UCLA, 1950).

Self-observation is not the same as introspection. Introspection means looking inside, examining your thoughts and feelings. Self-observation is a more objective process in which you examine your decisions and actions in situations where you did not make a conscious, value-based choice. It requires that you take occasional time out to reflect and then to notice patterns or themes. You can draw a "lifeline" and place markers at important decision points, or simply note each major decision point on a sticky note (actual or virtual) and then reflect on your decision-making process in each case. When patterns or themes emerge, you can consider questions like these:

- What was similar about those decisions or actions?

- What other options did I consider?

- Why was I attracted to the choice I made?

- Who or what influenced my choice?

- Would I make the same choice if faced with a similar situation today? Why, or why not?

Determining Internal Motivators

Motivation provides the energy that drives the choice, strength, and persistence of a behavior. The Latin root of the word *motivation* means "to move." Motivation is the crucial element in setting and attaining goals.

A motive is a need or desire to take action. We are motivated by both extrinsic (outside the self) and intrinsic (within the self) factors. Extrinsic factors can include

- tangible rewards such as bonuses

- approval or recognition

- relationships

- problems, or

- urgency.

Intrinsic factors can include

- achievement

- learning opportunity

- challenge

- moral imperative or value, or

- dissatisfaction with the status quo.

Two important theorists about human motivation are Abraham Maslow and Frederick Herzberg, who wrote in the 1950s and

1960s. Maslow[11], a psychologist, suggested that there was a hierarchy of human needs. He wrote that until needs at one level were satisfied, a person could not be motivated by higher-order needs. He displayed these needs as a pyramid. At the base level, we must have our physical needs satisfied; if we are hungry or exhausted or in pain, other needs seem irrelevant. Next, we are concerned for our own security and that of our family and community. Once we feel safe, we can be motivated by social needs—the desire to be loved and to belong to a group or community. Next our "ego needs" come into play; we want to think well of ourselves and to have others' respect and esteem. When all of these needs have been sufficiently met, we are motivated by what Maslow called "self-actualization." He described self-actualization as a person's need to be and do what he or she was born to be and do.

Herzberg[12] developed the "two factor" theory, in which he identified two dimensions that affect people's motivation at work. One dimension he called *hygiene factors*, which can be "job dissatisfiers" or de-motivators. The other dimension is *motivators*. When these needs are satisfied, higher-order work takes place. (Of course, people are very different as to the type and amount of fulfillment that satisfies their needs.) Hygiene factors include work conditions, salary, and interpersonal relations. Motivators include achievement, recognition, and opportunity for growth. Simply removing the negative hygiene factors is not enough to create motivation.

Using their insights, you can reflect on your current state of motivation. Is there something weighing you down, causing you to set your sights lower than you would like to? Perhaps you are more deeply concerned right now about practical, survival issues such as

---

11   Abraham Maslow, "A Theory of Human Motivation," *Psychological Review*, 1943
12   Frederick Herzberg, et al. *The Motivation to Work.* (John Wiley: New York, 1959)

making a living. Perhaps you are facing "demotivators" and you can't yet focus on what really drives you. Getting past these negative factors will provide the space to recognize your true motivators. Sometimes we have to close one door and step away from it before we can see the next one we want to enter. The classic works on transition by William Bridges[13] can help you to let go of the past and move toward an interesting future.

We often confuse inspiration and motivation. Inspiration is the power of moving the intellect or emotions to higher action through connecting to a person's intrinsic motivations. *Inspire* literally means to breathe in. The dictionary definition is "to fill with an animating…or exalting influence." Motivation is internal, but inspiration can also come from the outside, such as someone influencing you to take action by showing you what you could achieve. Most writers on leadership suggest that nobody can "motivate" another person. You can, however, *inspire* others or yourself by connecting a specific courageous or positive choice or action to powerful intrinsic motivators.

You may be motivated to take action in the West by either intrinsic or extrinsic factors. Anna was certainly motivated by the financial need her family was experiencing (extrinsic), but she was both motivated and inspired by her desire to help others succeed.

Another way to look at motivation is to identify what you experience as challenging, stimulating, and exciting. Fundamental to the skill of determining your primary motivators is a willingness to be deeply honest with yourself about this. What gets you up in the morning? What causes you to stay with a project or job even when it becomes difficult and frustrating or when other interesting

---

13 Bridges, William. *Transitions: Making Sense of Life's Changes*, Revised 25th Anniversary Edition, Boston: Da Capo Press, 2004

opportunities come along? What makes you want to learn something new or achieve something beyond anything you have done before? When you can answer those questions, you will understand the winds from the East that can fill your sails and drive you toward achieving your vision.

In this chapter, you have explored several approaches to learning about what moves you toward decisions and actions. Use the skills or approaches that you think will help to strengthen your driving forces and move you past the barriers that stand in the way of your eventual success.

Activities

1. If you have already developed a vision in the North, explore it using the Socratic Method (sometimes known as the "Five Whys") to climb down the Ladder of Inference.

    *   "Why do I want to go in that direction?

    *   "Why is that important to me?"

    *   Continue asking "why" questions until you begin to repeat yourself.

    *   Then ask, "What, specifically, do I see, hear, remember, or perceive that has led me to this conclusion?"

2. What are your three most important core values? Define them. Then, using the criteria cited above, test them by asking yourself:

    *   When and how did I realize that I had chosen these values as a motivating force instead of other alternatives?

    *   When and how have I stood up for these values by speaking out for them in a public way, even when it was not a popular position?

    *   When and how have I consciously applied these values to difficult and important decisions in my life? How am I applying them now?

3. Thinking back on the most important choice points in your life, what patterns or themes in your decisions have become apparent to you? What extrinsic and intrinsic motivations have guided your decisions?

4. What are the main drivers and motivators that guide your important life choices now? What challenges and inspires you as you think about your next choice points?

Chapter 10

The South

The South deals with our limitations and barriers—with all the factors that stop us from achieving our visions and living the life that we are capable of living. It is represented by the simple question "Why not?"

As you were going through the North section of the N.E.W.S.™ navigation model, you might have encountered your South—all the internal voices that argue why you should not take action. When we let ourselves envision something beyond our immediate reality, some negative internal voices may surface. Fears, hesitations, worries, insecurities—a host of limiting factors and barriers jostle for the right to be heard. These voices often get in the way of our realizing important visions and dreams. They might cause us to procrastinate, find excuses, or give up altogether on what we had hoped to achieve.

Often people are clear about what they really want (North), but they don't dare to go for it because of doubts or fears. We call this "being stuck in the South." In this situation, an individual remains less than the person he or she could become. Think of a baby chick in an egg. The eggshell provides the chick with shelter and security for a time. At some stage, the chick outgrows the shell, and the shell becomes a prison. The chick must find the power to crack the eggshell and free itself to move to the next space in order to survive. Likewise, we have limitations and fears; perhaps they are appropriate for a particular time in our lives. They keep us safe for a while. At some point, however, they become our prison and stop us from realizing our visions and dreams. In our case, the shell is usually self-manufactured; it is not physical, but in our mind. Whenever we come close to that barrier, we may feel weak and disempowered. It is as if we have hit an invisible but very real wall.

At times, after crossing or going beyond our boundaries and limitations, we look back and realize that it was only a virtual wall, a phantom. We might wonder why we waited. Breaking through the limitations of your South is a growth process. It means growing beyond your current limits, growing into a new domain of freedom to move, act, and express. It means moving to a domain in which your visions and dreams could come true. When liberating yourself from what holds you back in the South, you feel a release of energy, a sense of freedom—even joy.

To succeed in realizing our vision and goals, we first need to identify our South, our limiting barriers. Second, we need to choose to go beyond or through those barriers so they don't limit the possibilities of our life. Third, having chosen to grow past those limitations, we need to take action.

Limiting Factors

Limiting factors can arise from many origins. Some of them are natural—for example, justifiable caution in the face of real risk, such as a threat to one's physical being. However, many South factors are there because of messages that we received as children, such as "Never say what you really think; people might get hurt." Some injunctions come from parental or cultural influences, such as "You're not good enough. Why can't you be as successful as your brother?" or "People from this neighborhood never succeed." Some originate from our own experience, even if the experience is no longer relevant, such as "I tried to open a business once and failed miserably. I'm never going to do that again."

Limiting factors can also be external, such as a declining economy, problems in the family, or an abrasive boss. Different people view the same external factors differently and tell themselves a different story about them, leading to different feelings and a different set of actions and behaviors. So, even when the barriers seem to be external, our internal responses to them affect our power to handle them and make good decisions.

Barriers limit us, even if we are not fully conscious of them. They stop us from going where we want to go, frustrate us, and stand in the way of our success. Circus elephants are trained to stand in one place and not try to escape. When the elephant is small, the trainers tie its rear leg to a large peg stuck in the ground. The baby elephant spends hours trying to get away from that peg, but fails. This goes on day after day until it gives up the struggle. It's possible to tie a huge, mature elephant to a tiny peg in the ground if it has been trained in this way. It will not move. Reflecting on your own "training," what is the little peg that prevents you from moving freely?

Breaking Through

Moving or breaking through the limitations in your South is a process of personal growth. So, how do you break through limits? First, you have to identify them. That is not easy because, as the old Chinese saying goes, "The fish does not know it is in the water."

We identify with our beliefs, our barriers, and the stories we tell ourselves about reality. It's difficult to separate ourselves from them enough to identify and examine them so that we can choose whether we want to keep them or change them. Research shows that even the most intelligent people can hold on to irrational beliefs without examining them; they are just better at articulating and justifying them than those who are less intelligent.

The Diamond Model

The Diamond model can help in identifying your limiting barriers. It is a way of showing how we create our reality. We begin by *perceiving* a set of data. We unconsciously select the data and viewpoint that best fits our model of the world and respond to it with a *feeling* such as anger, excitement, embarrassment, or joy. We then *act* on that feeling and we *receive* a result that reinforces our perception, and the cycle begins anew.

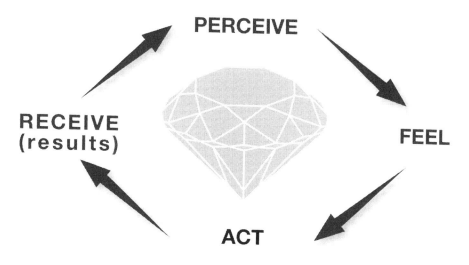

The model explains why different people can perceive the same reality differently. Three people might do the same job in the same company. One views it simply as a way to earn a living. The second views it as a great social environment with nice people. The third views the same job as a platform for promotion. They each feel differently about this job and about the time they spend doing it. The first might feel bored. The second might feel accepted and appreciated and take pleasure in being a good team player. The third might feel competitive and stressed. Of course, they will act and behave differently because of that. The first will probably do the minimum amount of work necessary to keep the job. The second will network with colleagues and teammates via e-mail or text or face to face in the office or the cafeteria. The third will take more and more responsibility, meet deadlines, and drive him or herself to succeed.

Eventually, each of the three people will achieve different results. The first will get a paycheck and go home, thinking that he or she is right that the job is all about making a living—and that is it. The second will have many contacts and friends and will believe that the job is all about relationships and contacts. The third will achieve business results and will measure himself or herself accordingly, thinking, *Yes, this is all about career development.* In this way, we interact with our world to create a certain reality through our own perceptions, feelings, and actions, reinforced by the responses we engender.

Changing Your Perceptions

We can recycle the same beliefs, assumptions, and perceptions again and again, and the results will be similar. How does a change in this perpetual process happen? One way is through a difficult or traumatic experience. Your perception of reality is shattered because something unexpected happens: a close friend dies, a partner decides to leave after you dedicated your life to him or her, your house burns down, or you have a heart attack. This is not a pleasant way to change your view of reality; but when something like that happens, it is unavoidable. We come to understand that we were wrong in our previous view—after all, there will be no exceptions made for us.

At this point, some people try to change their behavior, hoping for different results. ("From tomorrow I will start my exercise and diet program" or "I will keep my yard clear of brush" or "I will be nicer to the people I love.") This is like making a New Year's resolution. But to change a habitual behavior takes a great deal of discipline; most people can't really sustain it and they slide back to older, default habits. We can't change an application without changing the operating system that runs it.

Perhaps the best way to change our reality is to change the way we perceive it. The moment we view reality in a new way, we feel differently, we act differently, and eventually we get different results. This leads us to the actual work in the South. First, you identify the internal barrier, the limiting belief or story you tell yourself that stops you from achieving what you want. This can be done alone, although most people find it useful to work with someone else in this process. This allows you to confront your own attitudes and responses—things you can't see so easily by yourself. Here are examples of the type of questions to ask yourself:

- Why don't I do what I say I want to do?

- Why am I putting the action off? Why not do it now?

- What do I fear might happen if I take action?

- What external factors are stopping me?

- How am I stopping myself?

- What is the story I tell myself that blocks me?

- What do I say to myself when an opportunity for constructive action arises?

If you search deeply, you will eventually find a belief, an assumption, or an equation in your mind that is a limiting belief. It is the bug in your navigation system. Here are some examples from others who have done this type of work:

- "I am the only one who can do [my current job] well. I can't move on."

- "No one from my neighborhood [country, culture, race, gender, nationality, social class] can succeed at what I dream of doing."

- "I must work harder than anyone else to succeed."

- "Asking for more money [salary, fees] is too difficult."

- "I don't deserve more money [responsibility, etc.]."

- "I don't have the time for this."

- "I can't tell them what I really think."

- "It's too risky to be independent."

- "I can't trust anyone in my team."

- "I'm too busy to think about moving on."

- "I'm not good enough."

- "I'm too old to try something new."

- "If I leave the safety of this job, I will end up as a bag lady or like the homeless guys under the bridge."

- "My family is used to a certain standard of living. I can't risk it."

As you can see, these beliefs—in the form of self-talk—are expressed by a simple sentence or phrase that come up when we consider moving forward toward achieving our vision. Becoming aware of what we tell ourselves to stop this forward progress is essential. This type of internal work is not psychotherapy. Rather, it is self-study. We identify barriers and find ways to go beyond them to realize our visions and goals. It's very much in the spirit of Einstein's famous quote "The significant problems we face cannot be solved by the same level of thinking we were at when we created them."

Once you recognize a limiting belief, you need to choose whether you want to change it. It won't be comfortable at first; it will take some serious work. You need to make that choice consciously and of your free will. If you don't like the results that limiting belief has created in the past or present, or what it might mean for your future, you can choose to do something about it. This approach creates readiness that can allow for choice and change. We can tolerate awful situations by adapting to them on a day-to-day basis, but when confronted with the price we have paid over the years and the price we might have to pay in the years to come, we may come to the point of making a different choice.

Questions

1. What is the main limiting belief that has been a barrier to achieving what you are capable of and dream of achieving?

2. Using the Diamond model, consider how that belief operates to create and reinforce this barrier. Explore your emotional response to the limiting belief when you express it to yourself. Then explore how it stimulates you to act or behave in many situations. What kind of results do you receive from acting and behaving in this way? What results has it brought you in the last few years, both internally and with others? What results does it offer you now? Lastly, if you maintain this belief, this feeling, and the actions based on it, what results will it give you over the next ten years?

3. If you choose the path of exploring and perhaps getting rid of the limiting belief, what could you do that would test or allow you to modify that belief or assumption?

4. What alternative belief or assumption might be realistic, given the facts of the situation, and yet allow you greater freedom to move toward your vision?

Michael

Michael Lazarus, thirty-eight, has been considered a high performer at the Fortune 100 company where he has worked for the past five years. Since Michael was a young child, he has been told that he has "leadership qualities." He was deeply involved with scouting, community, and school activities. In high school and college, he was considered a "big man on campus" and had many friends and admirers. He breezed through university with a B average and received a business degree. There were many offers to choose from, and he took a series of increasingly well-paid and responsible middle-management jobs in high-tech firms. Michael believes that he has the qualities required to become a senior leader.

Recently, a new manager took the place of his very supportive boss, who was promoted and moved to a different division. The new manager has an engineering background. This manager does not seem to respect Michael's business and financial savvy; it seems as if he respects only people with technical backgrounds like his own. He tends to micromanage Michael and others on the team who are not engineers.

Michael is offended by this. He feels disrespected and often comes to work with a negative attitude, expecting to be treated with condescension. He is very hesitant to open up this issue with the new manager; he worries about the consequences of such a discussion. His results at work are diminishing after so many years of success. Michael gets depressed more and more often. His peers start to wonder what happened to someone who was once the "wonder boy" of the department. His partner encourages him to look elsewhere, as the work issues are beginning to affect Michael at home.

Michael calls a friend who has recently completed training in a course for managers on coaching their teams. At the coffee shop where they meet the next day, Bob says, "I can't really take you on as a coaching client, because I only have tools to coach my own team at work. But I'm happy to walk you through the process, and if you want me to, I can recommend someone to work with you to take a deeper dive."

"Anything would be helpful at this point," Michael replies. "I'm trying to stay positive, but I've never had a manager who didn't respect me and appreciate my work. I can't see how I can stay in the company and get the support and chance for promotion that I was expecting. I wonder if I can even make it in any high-tech company now. This guy will certainly not be a positive reference for me." *Michael drums his fingers on the table and looks down. His forehead is creased, and he slumps back in his chair.*

Bob asks, "So what are you most concerned about?"

Michael releases a sigh and says, "My manager doesn't appreciate me and my experience at all. He micromanages me, and my results are going downhill fast."

"So?"

"Well, he might fire me eventually, and I will end up with no job at my age. You know how it is in this industry."

Bob sums it up: "So, you believe that if this goes on you will not have a job in the IT industry. And?"

Michael furrows his brow. He slumps further down in his chair. "Well, you know how hard I worked for it. I really don't want to end up like my father—sitting at home, out of shape, bored, and unemployed."

Bob pulls a diamond-shaped chart out of his briefcase. "Here's what I see," *he says, pointing to the top of the chart, at the word* 'Perceive.' "You believe your manager has a preference for people with technical backgrounds. You hear him make a comment about your work, and you believe you might lose your job and be without an income and end up like your father. *Bob moves his finger around the chart, to the word* 'Feel.' You feel unappreciated and disempowered." *Michael nods in acknowledgement.*

Bob then points to the word 'Act.' "You let him make a decision that you should have made. Even though you're angry and frustrated, you don't speak up or do anything about it."

Finally, Bob taps his finger next to the word 'Receive.' "So, what result does your behavior have?"

"Well," says Michael, showing some insight, " I guess he assumes I have nothing to say and that justifies his micromanagement."

"And this reinforces your feelings of worthlessness in the situation. Do I have that right?"

"That's a pretty accurate description of my work life these days. You always had a knack for reading my mind." Michael manages a half-hearted grin. "I don't think I know how to break that cycle. Maybe I should just give up here and go back to graduate school. I wasn't that great a student, though—I'm not confident that I could get into a good MBA program."

"It sounds to me as if you need to work through some of your issues and barriers before you make any long-term decisions," Bob says. You don't feel confident about pushing back with your boss or moving on in the industry, and you don't believe you can get into a good program if you leave for further education. There's a kind of vicious circle going on here.

"Maybe you should work for a while with my coach, Sally. She's been doing this for a while, and I think she might be able to help you. She'll examine your limiting beliefs with you and find a way to move beyond them and break through this vicious circle. You can work together to devise a plan that can create a different and better reality for you. Would you like to have her cell number? I know she has helped many people in similar situations."

Michael takes Sally's number as he starts to feel some hope for the first time in weeks.

Skills for the South

When you deal with the South, your work will focus on identifying and overcoming barriers. Some useful skills in doing this involve critical thinking and problem solving. These include

- identifying and testing assumptions

- risk assessment, and

- risk adjustment.

Uncovering and Testing Assumptions

The South is full of unexamined assumptions. Fears may be assumptions that something bad will happen if you take certain actions. One of the keys to breaking through fears is the ability to take a temporarily neutral stance toward your own assumptions. This enables you to test their basis in fact as opposed to opinions, preferences, habits, or vested interests as well as their limiting effect on your thinking. What solutions or opportunities are you not considering due to unexamined assumptions?

People frequently hold unexamined assumptions concerning:
- the definition of the problem or opportunity

- who or what caused—or is responsible for—the current situation

- their own talents and abilities

- the consequences of taking action

- where the solution to a problem lies;

- how to approach an opportunity, or

- their ability to influence the course of events.

Our vested interests (what we have to gain or lose) influence our thinking and decision making. It's important to bring those interests into our conscious awareness in order not to fall into the "wishful thinking" trap. This trap awaits those who assume that the easiest path or the path that would produce the best outcome for them is also the most intelligent and strategic choice. When we operate from our fears, we may decide that avoidance of an action is the safest course. We then defend that decision to ourselves and to others as wise, given the circumstances.

You or another person can usually uncover your assumptions by asking questions like these:

- "What stops me from moving forward with this? Why don't I do what I say I want to do?"

- "What is hindering my progress? Why don't I act now?"

- "What might happen if I tried to take action? What's my worst-case scenario? What do I fear?"

- "What external factors are stopping me? How do I know that to be true?"

- "How am I stopping myself?"

- "What's the story I tell myself that blocks me? What do I say to myself when an opportunity for constructive action arises?"

Once you're aware of your assumptions, you can identify the issues over which you have control as well as those that are outside your direct control but which will have an impact on the outcome you're working toward. You can then decide how to address them. If, for example, you have a fear of taking a particular action based on a previous experience, you can examine the factual basis of that fear with the following questions:

- What is the frequency of the negative outcome in relation to the number of times the action is carried out (by me or others)?

- How is this outcome relevant to me? What negative results could occur? What positive results might occur if I experienced and confronted the resulting situation?

- What is the worst possible outcome (informed by the frequency and type of negative outcomes)?

- What would I do if the worst happens?

- What skills would I need in order to address that worst-case situation in a positive way?

You can also examine how the fear may be limiting your choices.

- What actions would I take if I didn't fear the result?

- What actions would I take if I expected a positive result (in other words, if I assumed the opposite of the fear or belief)?

- What successful actions have other people in my situation taken?

- If I knew that I could not fail, what would I do?

If the assumption is concerning something you have no control over, such as the economy or large-scale organizational change, consider how to take actions that would ameliorate the situation. We will discuss this further in the section on risk assessment and adjustment.

As Michael works with his coach, Sally, they identify a number of assumptions that he is making. These are among them:

- *His boss doesn't respect him because he is not an engineer.*

- *It's not okay to push back with the boss.*

- *If he loses this job, he won't be able to get another one in the industry.*

- *He would not be able to gain entry to a good MBA program.*

Sally takes each of the assumptions in turn and asks Michael to give her the evidence for the conclusion. Then she asks him to give her some contradictory evidence for each. They find that there is little hard data to support some of his assumptions.

"Which of these assumptions are you willing to test and examine more closely, Michael?" she asks.

"I think I have the least evidence about pushing back—but I'm not willing to go very far with it."

"Let's try a 'baby steps' experiment. Are you willing to try pushing back—just a little—the next time he overrides your decision? Maybe ask him to explain why he did it?"

Michael agrees to the experiment and slowly, over time, he and Sally work through each of his major assumptions. Many of his experiments succeed, and he gets bolder. Each time he disproves an assumption, his confidence grows, and his fears diminish. One or two of them test as true, and he and Sally devise a plan to change his approach in a way that allows him to move forward around the barrier rather than to push through it. For example, he signs up for some online courses to help improve his readiness for graduate school.

Examining your own assumptions is difficult, though not impossible, to do alone. If you can, engage a coach, a trusted colleague, or a friend to work with you by asking tough questions like these about your assumptions:

- How do you know that to be true? What evidence do you have?

- What alternative explanations might fit the same facts that you have observed?

- What would you do if you didn't believe that to be the case?

- What's the worst thing that could happen if you tried it? What would you do in response?

Risk Assessment

Whenever you set off on a journey or an adventure—something you have never done before—there will be risk. You wouldn't start on any great adventure without making sure that you had what you needed to get you there and back safely. You would want to be certain that you knew where you were going and had a map and plan for getting there. You would want to have the best possible crew. You'd spend time with them discussing possible problems or dangers and how to avoid or minimize them. You would also look at ways to maximize the rewards of the journey. You would anticipate that an emergency could happen, and you would bring along what you might need in case it did.

Navigating your life is your greatest adventure, so it's reasonable to anticipate that you will face risks. The dictionary definition of risk is "the possibility of loss or injury." From our point of view, risk-taking means moving to action when

- the outcome is not known or easily predictable, and

- there is the possibility of a loss or of negative consequences.

We take some risks, regardless, because taking the risk offers an opportunity for a more positive outcome than could be achieved otherwise.

The courage involved in doing something bold creates great opportunities. As the Greek historian Herodotus said in 484 BCE, "Great deeds are wrought at great risk." In 1961, President John F. Kennedy said, "I believe this nation should commit itself, to achieving the goal, before this decade is out, of landing a man on the moon and returning him safely to the earth." A great risk, indeed.

Not all risks are worth taking, of course. You won't get through the South without taking some risks, but they should be intelligent risks. What is an intelligent risk? It meets the following criteria:

- The potential gain is worth the potential loss. Taking the risk will enable you to break through previous limitations.

- The risk is well considered; implications and consequences have been thought through.

- The level of risk is actively managed, not just a toss of the coin. The odds are in your favor to begin with, or you have adjusted risk factors to increase the probability of success or decrease the probability of negative consequences.

Even the most intelligent risk taking will sometimes end in failure. But failed risks are worthwhile: you can learn from the experience and gain confidence and strength from pushing past your limits. Often, much more is learned from a risk that failed than from one that succeeded, as many scientists and inventors can attest. "Fail early, fail often" is a mantra for success in innovation that can be applied to your life's journey. A willingness to experiment in low-cost ways will serve you well as you navigate through the South.

If you have a clear vision of success or a plan; you can assess the risks you face by asking yourself what might stop you from achieving your vision or what could go wrong with your plan. You also need to consider all the positive results that you hope to achieve through taking a particular risk. Mathematical risk models could be useful in some cases, but most of the risks you will face on your journey will not have engendered a great deal of relevant data that you can look up. You'll have to make some educated guesses.

In assessing risks, it's important to distinguish between a realistic risk and a faulty assumption or fear. Your skills in examining and testing assumptions will be useful here. You explore the factors that will affect the outcome of your move to action—the possible gains and losses—so you can take steps to increase the probability of success or modify your approach so you can go around any barriers.

As you probably noticed in Michael's case, he perceived the act of pushing back with his manager to be very risky. His plan with Sally involved first assessing and later adjusting the risks to the point that the potential positive factors outweighed the negative ones. For example, he identified the following risks as being especially important:

- *His manager might fire him.*

- *He might not be able to find another job that would enable him to use his talents and to grow.*

Acknowledging what he was afraid of made room for Michael to begin thinking of the positive side – what he might gain by taking action.

- *His manager might gain respect for him and stop micromanaging.*

- *He might gain greater self-respect.*

- *He might feel more confident about applying for other jobs or graduate school and could achieve a good result.*

Often there is a dialogue between your East and your South. Voices from the East will encourage you to move on according to your core drivers, your intuition, and your dreams. Voices from the South will point out the risks and tell you to be fearful of the consequences. To be successful as a self-navigator, you need to listen to your East while assessing the relevance of the voices you hear from the South and then making decisions and taking action in the West.

Risk Adjustment

Sometimes when we have assessed the risks involved in pushing past our limiting beliefs and fears, we are daunted and hesitant. The costs and the benefits don't seem to balance out. When we feel this way, we *dis*courage ourselves—in other words, we lose our courage. Instead, we can empower ourselves to take action through adjusting the risks. As an intelligent risk taker, you can identify modifications or changes that will affect the overall level of risk in the situation. You can make the risk more acceptable and manageable so that you take action with greater confidence and courage. You can actually *en*courage yourself.

Risks that are taken voluntarily and wholeheartedly produce better results than ones taken tentatively or reluctantly.

Risk can be adjusted in two directions: decreasing potential loss and increasing potential gain. In addition, successful risk adjustment changes the overall "economics" of the risk enough to increase your own motivation to take the risk. To modify risk levels, you improve the quality of the probable outcome by reducing costs, increasing benefits, or decreasing the probability of the worst-case scenario occurring. In these ways, you can change both the external reality and your internal perceptions of risk.

Here are several different approaches to adjusting risk. You can take one or several of the following actions:

- Gather information. The more you know, the more prepared you will be and the greater the possible control you will have over the outcome.

- Increase influence. Find the key actors in the situation and get to know them; form mutual influence relationships.

- Decrease exposure. Through these relationships, get others to share the risk with you. The insurance industry is based on the fact that the more people who are exposed to a risk, the less risk each person carries.

- Consider time. You may be able to "buy" more of it. Many things that seem urgent can be pushed back, allowing you time to learn, influence, practice, and take other actions to decrease your vulnerability to the downside of a specific risk. On the other hand, you may increase the risks you face if you fail to act in a timely way.

- Develop alternatives. Knowing what to do in the worst case can give you courage to move forward. Create a set of possible scenarios and ways to respond.

- Learn or improve skills. Identify what you need to be able to do to be more successful and find a way to develop and practice that skill.

- Gain support or tangible resources. Influence others to become part of your team; ask them to provide what you need to succeed in exchange for tangible or intangible benefits. Ask others to encourage you, to cheer you on.

- Bite off smaller "chunks" of action. Take some baby steps toward your goal.

- Diversify. Try parallel paths to the same result. If you fail at one, perhaps another will succeed.

Research by Gabriele Oettingen of New York University suggests that "mentally contrasting a desired future with present reality leads to the emergence of binding goals with consecutive goal striving and goal attainment, as long as chances of success are perceived to be high." In other words, "double thinking" about your goal in contrast to the present reality, and then identifying barriers and imagining how you might overcome them, is more likely to lead to successful goal attainment than focusing on the vision or the difficulties alone. As Michael prepares for his "baby step" action of pushing back with his boss, it would be helpful for him to envision himself behaving in a self-confident way with his manager, then contrasting that to his present behavior. He might then imagine various issues that could arise when he tries the new behavior and envision himself overcoming each barrier successfully. In this way he prepares for success while planning in a realistic and practical way to handle any difficulties. Facing and planning for the "worst case" adds to his confidence and increases the likelihood that he will succeed.

> *As Michael and Sally work together, they identify several ways he could adjust the risks. One of the major ones involves finding out where other jobs in his field are available and matching his credentials with the requirements. He might even consider going out on one or two job interviews to see how he is received. That would give him greater confidence that he could deal with the worst case. He could also rehearse a conversation with his manager; Sally offers to play it out with him and give him some feedback. Having these possible activities in mind make the balance of risk and reward more attractive and can propel him to the action that he needs to take in order to move forward.*

There are some actions that you will take regardless of the risks involved. These actions occur when the motivation from your East is so powerful that it carries you past the barriers of the South. The motivation can come in the form of a strong desire to achieve your vision or in compelling values that will not allow you to give in to your fears. I have often heard people say, when describing a great risk they have taken, "I could not *not* do it." They felt a thrilling sense of achievement and power at facing and overcoming their fears. Those are often the proudest moments of our lives. For most of us, most often, there is time for a thoughtful assessment and adjustment of the risks involved in breaking through the obstacles of the South to the West, where action takes place.

Activities

1. What are the major concerns or barriers that come up for you as you think about moving toward action to achieve your vision?

2. What might you be assuming to support each of these concerns, fears, or limiting beliefs? How do you know these assumptions to be true? What would you do if you did not have them?

3. Identify the major risks involved in moving forward.

4. Assess each of them through a thoughtful cost-and-benefit analysis. What could go wrong? On the other hand, what could you achieve through taking this risk that you could not achieve without it?

5. Choose two or three of the cost factors, and ask how you could adjust them to reduce the downside risk or to create a soft landing. Then consider how you could increase the probability of success or the benefits of taking action.

6. Identify the motivating factors from your East that will give you the courage to overcome your reluctance and take bold action regardless of the risks involved. Once you make a decision and take action, how will that help you to grow?

7. Hold your vision of success in your mind, together with the anticipated risks and barriers. Imagine yourself confronting each of these successfully. Summarize in writing the vision you hope to achieve and how you will handle specific difficulties that you can expect to occur.

.

Chapter 11

The West

The West in the N.E.W.S.™ navigation model relates to the question, "How will you get to where you want to go?" The West has two key components: planning and execution. Planning is everything we do to prepare for moving to action, and execution is how we actually do it.

Being stuck in the West means that you might be clear about your North direction, you are well connected to the drivers in your East, and you have worked out the barriers in your South—yet you find it difficult to move to action. Even with all your hard work and good intentions, your vision is not materializing. This leads to feelings of failure and frustration.

The work in the West is very practical. It has to do with bringing order out of chaos, creating a good plan that includes resources, people, and events to allow for successful execution. Like any other kind of project management, the work moves from the overall view in the North to a very detailed view in the West, including deliverables, milestones, and timeline.

In the West, we must make sure that we have the right skills and that we know how to manage resources and get other people on board so they will support us, provide resources, and take part in the execution of our plan. Most importantly, to be successful in the West, we need discipline and focus. We live in an age when many things compete for our attention. We feel the need to be available to everyone, through all our media, most of the time. Everything seems to require an immediate response. We suffer from urgency fatigue.

Dave, a foundation executive I met recently, told me how he wakes up in the morning and while still in bed looks at his smartphone for the latest e-mails, tweets, and Facebook messages. On the way to the office and throughout the day, he is connected and available. He is constantly living in his inbox. By 6:00 p.m., he is exhausted and yet feels he has not done one single important thing that day. Even at the family dinner table, he stays connected to and engaged with the world outside rather than being with his spouse and children.

Many people these days find it difficult to concentrate for more than a few minutes. A common disease of the early-twenty-first century might be called "acquired attention deficit disorder." In moving from one task to the next, we suffer context switches, causing us to lose focus for a few minutes each time, many times over each day. Like Dave, we can't seem to find time to do the things that are important for us. The North is forgotten in the middle of all this swirling, yet often-trivial, urgency. We are hyperactive, but fail to achieve our vision and goals.

This is an ongoing reality for many of us. The work in the West is designed to focus you on activities that are worthwhile to invest in—the ones that will create your desired future. It's a question of return on investment—which activities will give you the greatest return on your allotment of time, money, energy, and other resources? Ideally, you will invest in the high-leverage activities that will create the future that you want in the long run.

You should take three steps in the West. The first is to set critical short-term goals to create a focus that will allow you to harness your resources and achieve your vision. Critical goals are those very few goals that you must achieve in the coming year so your vision can come true. If you want to practice law, you need to go to law school. It is not a good idea or "nice to have" if you wish to be admitted to the bar. A critical goal, then, would be to gain admission to law school.

As you review your vision and think about the coming year, you will probably realize that there are many things to do if you are going to move forward. You'll need to narrow them to a short list; the ones that must be achieved in the coming year. These critical goals need to be strategic, realistic, attainable, and within your sphere of influence.

The second step is to break down these critical goals to a list of all the activities and resources needed to achieve them. If this is a new area for you, it might be a good idea to get the help or involvement of someone who has "been there and done that." Not all of the items on your list will have the same priority. Some of them are essential. Some of them are important. And some of them are just nice to have. At this stage, you need to focus on the essentials. You will then use them to create a tactical plan. In ancient Greek, the word for tactics, *taktika*, means activities that pertain to some sort of arrangement or order—a step-by-step plan of progression. This is what you will do in the West—create a plan for the year, month by month, that will enable you to achieve your critical goals.

There are two processes involved in creating a strong tactical plan. One is "retro-planning," and the other is "dependencies analysis." Retro-planning has to do with planning from the desired end back to the present. If you're taking a trip abroad, you consider how much time you need before the trip to get a passport or a visa. Later, you decide how soon you will need to pack. When you apply dependencies analysis, you identify what depends on what in your plan. For example, you need a passport before you apply for a visa. Using these two processes, you can create a year-long plan that specifies the high priority activities and resources you will need in order to achieve your desired result.

Third, you'll develop a weekly plan of activities. As you move through the year, it's not enough to have a yearly or monthly plan. You need to have a weekly set of goals. This allows you to actualize your plan. Imagine that you are operating in a deep forest. Take a break each week from your activities on the floor of the forest—where the action takes place—and climb a tree. From that elevated view, revisit your long-term vision and yearly goals and then define or redefine weekly activities that will move these goals forward. A few specific activities will be the best investment of your time in the following week.

You have probably heard of the 80/20 principle. Vilfredo Pareto, an early-twentieth-century Italian economist, outlined this principle. He discovered that 80 percent of the land was owned by 20 percent of the population. This distribution of wealth recurred throughout the ages in many different countries. Later economists named this 80/20 distribution "the Pareto principle," and it seems to hold true across many different contexts. Every week, you can focus on the 20 percent of activities that will create 80 percent of the results that you want to achieve. In this way, you'll make the most effective use of your time and resources.

This will help you focus in the midst of the many things that need to happen that week. It's important to schedule these "20 percent" activities and tell someone else about your plan; this accountability makes it more likely that you will actually do them. For example, it's much more likely that you'll go to the gym if you have a personal appointment with a fitness instructor. Just having a membership may not be enough, since you're only accountable to yourself as to how much you use it.

When your plan is focused, sequential, and ready to execute, you'll be aware that achieving it will requires a great deal of discipline. You may need to learn skills that you don't have now. You will certainly need to focus on specific tasks that you can commit to do. You will have to find ways to stay on track.

As you work in the West, key events will be major building blocks in your execution. Prepare well for those important events. Consider rehearsing those events before they happen and get feedback from someone who is willing to help you prepare. Politicians, celebrities, and senior leaders of large enterprises nearly always rehearse for important events (speeches, interviews, debates, public appearances, key meetings) with a coach or key advisors. Those who don't do this often live to regret it.

Questions:

1. To what degree do you currently make a conscious plan to achieve your goals?

2. If so, to what degree do you follow your plan and/or adjust it based on changing circumstances?

Julio

Julio Gonzales, twenty-three, has just graduated from a good university with an MBA, specializing in finance. He has realized in the last year or so that, while he is very good at the financial side of business, the thought of becoming a CPA or corporate financial person is not very exciting. At heart, he is a musician who chose what he and his immigrant parents saw as a safe path to a comfortable future. Now he is facing the reality of the world of work. Should he take a job for which he is qualified and try it for a few years? Should he delay his entry into the corporate world and see if he can make money with his music? That would probably end the way his last band did—a lot of friends' weddings and a few gigs at the local pubs, which were all pass-the-hat propositions.

Julio calls his college counselor, Rae, who has become a friend over the past few years. He thinks maybe she will have some ideas for him or at least be a sounding board as he thinks through his next steps. They agree to meet in the lobby of the student union. Julio carries a cup of coffee to the comfortable chairs in the corner of the large space where Rae is already settled.

"Hi, Julio. It's been a few months. Congratulations on getting your degree."

"Thanks, Rae. I'm glad to be finished with it, but now I'm trying to figure out where to go from here. It all seemed pretty simple a few years ago—get a good degree, get hired at a good firm, then settle down, get married, have kids, buy a house. You know, the American dream. My parents wanted all of us to achieve it."

"And now you're not sure it's your dream?"

"Right—as you usually are, Rae. You know that I've always loved music. I guess if I didn't have to worry about money, I'd be trying my

luck in New York or LA or even New Orleans. Jazz is really my passion, but I love all kinds of music—Latin, hip-hop, rock, folk."

"You don't sound like someone who's ready to take your CPA exam, Julio."

He smiles. "I'm beginning to hatch an idea, Rae. I might go ahead and take that exam, but I don't want to go to work on Wall Street or for a tax accounting firm. I'd like to help musicians make a buck and keep it. If there's anything I know about musicians, it's that most of them know nothing about money. It's not that they want to be poor; it's just that they haven't a clue how to make money, keep it, or put it to work."

"So it sounds as if you know what you were born to do, Julio, and what you're passionate about. You sound determined—as if you know exactly where you're heading. Do you have a practical model and vision?"

"I think I do. I will set up a small agency specializing in working with young musicians. It will have an emphasis on saving and investing some of their income. Once I have fifteen to twenty customers, I'll be able to run a self-sustaining business.

"That sounds exciting," Rae says. "I think the question for you is how you're going to make it work."

"I guess I need some kind of a business plan. Luckily, I had to take a course in that. I guess my education had some benefits, but I'm not sure how to start."

Rae smiles and says, "How about starting by setting goals for the coming year—goals that let you focus on what's really important to achieve on the way to actualizing your personal vision."

"Of course. You're absolutely right; I need to get into the market soon. If I want to be known as a solution provider, I'll have to get my proposal for musicians ready. I want to have my first three musician customers by the end of this year so I can get some word-of-mouth advertising started

in that world." Rae nods in agreement, and Julio goes on with enthusiasm in his voice "Now I can break it down to an activity plan." Julio pulls out his smartphone and starts making notes.

"Don't forget a good contact list if you want to enter the world of professional musicians," Rae adds. She realizes that he's starting to create a plan to move his initiative forward.

Julio leaves their meeting with greater determination and a sense of clarity about his next steps. Rae waves at him and smiles as she thinks," If anyone can create a successful combination of music and money management, it will be Julio."

Skills for the West

Now you are ready for action. Putting your plan to work will involve many skills. Some of them are

- setting critical goals

- scenario planning, and

- influencing and negotiating with others.

Setting Critical Goals

One of the major challenges in the West is the challenge of focus. To gain greater control and focus, we must be able to set critical goals and identify activities to achieve them. There are many types of goals, but very few of them are critical. To set critical goals, the first step is to consider your vision and then ask yourself what must be achieved this year so that you can make serious advances toward actualizing the vision. You can then make an extended list of possible goals, which are actual results or outcomes that you need to achieve. You may want to invite someone you trust to help you develop this list.

Next, look at these goals through several prisms, based on your criteria for success. For example, examine each one according to its economic impact, its impact on your well-being, and its impact on others you are involved with. Finally, consider how important each goal is to achieving your plan.

During this process, some additional goals will probably surface. You're searching for your critical goals, the few goals that will answer all of your requirements. The discipline of focus requires that you have very few critical goals at any given time—probably no more than two or three. It's important to post them in places that you see often (for example, your computer, the first screen on your mobile device, your car dashboard, the inside of your front door, your bathroom mirror) and then to plan your activities on a weekly and monthly basis accordingly. To make these critical goals real and driving for you, set measures of success for each goal. Ask yourself,

- What will success look like if I succeed in achieving this goal?

- What will I see, hear, or experience that will let me know it has been accomplished?

- How will I measure it?

Setting and acting on critical goals will give you a great deal of focus and a better chance of steering the course of your life through the storm of activities that go on around you.

Scenario Planning

Scenario planning was devised by the military as a method for planning campaigns. By the 1970s, it was being applied in business by companies such as Royal Dutch Shell, which used it to look for events that might affect oil prices. Scenario planning offers individuals or groups a way to question assumptions and see reality in a different and more productive way, enabling them to prepare for a future they can't entirely control. Peter Schwartz[14] has written extensively about how organizations use this approach. Here we'll apply it to individuals.

Scenario planning involves imagining and even exaggerating several possible scenarios based on factors that are outside of one's control. Successful scenario planners seek input on possible futures from a variety of sources—often from unusual people and outside-the-box thinkers. Most importantly, they seek input from people who don't think the same way that they do. This is the key to using scenario planning effectively. With the search tools that are readily available to us now, we can seek a broad range of opinion about the future that is relevant to our goals and visions. However, it's imperative to look outside our own comfort zone for respected thinkers and researchers who may see the world differently. Recent research suggests, rather chillingly, that smart people don't necessarily base their opinions on better data; rather, they are better at coming up with a rationale for opinions they already hold.

There are many ways to approach individual scenario planning. Schwartz suggests that scenarios often fall into three categories and that three scenarios is a good number for a planning session:

- Growth scenario: more of the same, but better

- Decay or devastation scenario: change for the worse

- Opportunity scenario: disruptive but potentially positive shift

---

14   Peter Schwartz, *The Art of the Long View* (**New York**: Currency Doubleday, 1996).

There are three elements to planning scenarios:

- Key factors: What will have an impact on the future of your problem, issue, or opportunity that you are not in control of?

- Plots: How might those factors play out in a growth, decay, or opportunity scenario? The decay and opportunity scenarios suggest more extreme outcomes of these independent factors.

- Implications: What would you need to do to succeed or at least survive in each one of those scenarios?

Reality is likely to be different from any of the scenarios. However, by planning for each of them and staying out of the wishful-thinking mode, you will be better prepared for whatever happens. Remember, success does not depend merely on the way the key factors play out, but on the way you prepare and respond. By doing this work, you create the basis for practical and realistic alternative plans as events occur and the situation develops.

A few days after Julio's initial conversation with Rae, after he has done some initial analysis and planning, they meet again to consider some possible scenarios. They begin by listing factors that Julio needs to consider—things he is not able to control. They come up with a list that includes, among others;

- *the economy*

- *competitors—are there or could there be other people with the same specialty?*

- *the market for music—will there be musicians who have money that they need and want to be managed?*

They decide to develop just two scenarios. The ideal scenario is that the economy comes roaring back; musicians find ways to make money from their work through selling their music and tickets to their concerts; and few, if any, competitors have a similar background. The other scenario assumes that the economy goes into a recession; there are many experienced money managers and advisers scrambling to work with the few musicians who manage to remain successful; and most young musicians have to sleep under a bridge and play in subway stations, hoping for change to be thrown into their hat. Julio and Rae deliberately exaggerate both scenarios to stimulate their thinking.

"So, what would you do in the first case, Julio?"

"I already started to think about this possibility. I'd plan to live on my savings for a few months. My first move would be to expand my network of musician friends and acquaintances, pick two or three to be my "beta" customers, and ask them to let their friends know about my work if they like it. I would help them plan, invest, and manage their money for, say, six months. I wouldn't charge them anything for that, though they would have to agree to make a contract after that time if they want to continue. At the same time, I'd hire someone to develop a website, using music from my friends and even some of my own—maybe offering some free downloads for people who add their name to my mailing list..." Julio went on discussing his plan for the optimistic scenario. It sounded reasonable to Rae.

"How about the second scenario? What would you do then?"

"The first thing I'd have to do is move back home to save money. I'd still do the networking and build a website, but I'd have to do it myself. There are a lot of free tools for doing that. It wouldn't be as professional, but it would work. I'd start small by offering to help musicians budget the little bit of money they have. I might even start something on my website that would connect people so they could pool their money to buy sound equipment and other things they could share."

As Julio continued imagining the worst-case scenario, he realized that a number of the ideas he came up with could work regardless of what happened to the economy or the fate of the music business. These ideas would probably give him an advantage over money managers who didn't understand musicians. He left the meeting full of enthusiasm and ready to get down to work.

Influencing and Negotiating with Others[15]

Whatever you plan to do, it's unlikely that you'll be able to accomplish it alone. At some point in your journey, you'll need the support and resources that others can provide. You'll also need a good set of influence skills. *Influence* means getting something done through others. In contrast to manipulation, which is an unfair or hidden attempt to manage others' behavior or choices, influence is done openly; the other person is always responsible for making the choice to act.

---

15 Some material adapted with permission from *Exercising Influence: Building Relationships and Getting Results*, Barnes & Conti Associates, 1994, 2012, and *Constructive Negotiation*, Barnes & Conti Associates, 1994, 2012

Influence is more than good communication. Communication moves information from one mind to another. Influence moves ideas into action; it produces an effect without the use of force or command. You can communicate without influencing, but you can't influence without communicating. Influence behaviors are intended to result in action by another party or parties.

Some people confuse influence with power. We define *power* as a set of resources that you have and *influence* as a set of skills or actions that puts your power to work. Influence is the act of moving another person toward action without the use of direct power or authority. Most of the people whose help you will need on your journey will not have to do what you ask of them if they don't want to. In general, people feel influenced when they are treated with respect and fairness and are offered a choice. That approach is the most likely to succeed.

There are many ways to influence others; some are direct and some are indirect. In this chapter, we will deal primarily with direct influence, whether in a face-to-face, voice-to-voice, or electronic format.

Being an effective influencer requires more than intellectual understanding, of course. It takes a great deal of practice and feedback, which will enable you to develop the skills you underuse and develop a thoughtful influence strategy focused on your goals and objectives.

Influence skills are directional. Sometimes you want to send your ideas, offers, requirements, or visions toward others. We call those behaviors "expressive influence." Sometimes you want to stimulate the other person to give you information, ideas, trust, or commitments. This we call "receptive influence."

Expressive influence includes the following tactics and behaviors:

- Tell: Communicate the desired action by making suggestions or expressing needs.

- Sell: Convince the other to commit to action through offering reasons or referring to goals and benefits.

- Negotiate: Give the other a vested interest in taking the action through offering incentives or describing consequences.

- Enlist: Create enthusiasm and alignment through envisioning success or encouraging.

Receptive influence consists of these tactics and behaviors:

- Inquire: Get information and guide thinking by asking open-ended questions or drawing the other person out.

- Listen: Learn about, reinforce, or expand the other's thinking through checking understanding or testing implications.

- Attune: Build trust or increase openness through identifying with the other or disclosing information.

- Facilitate: Help the other to accept responsibility for taking action through clarifying issues or posing challenging questions.

Your influence strategy with anyone should be built on an understanding of three different areas:

- Your goal or intention—what you want the other person to do:
    - o What is your long-term goal or vision?
    - o What action do you want the other person to take that will help you to achieve this?
    - o What can you observe during the influence conversation that will let you know that you are making progress in gaining the other's commitment to action?

- The state of your influence relationship with the other person:
    - o Do you have a positive, two-way influence relationship with him or her now?
    - o Is there anything from the past that needs to be addressed or repaired before your influence can succeed?

- The context at the time your influence action takes place:
    - o What is important to this individual? What are his or her values, goals, or vested interests?
    - o What is his or her personality like? How does she or he prefer to be approached?
    - o How does he or she make decisions? What kind of information or action is most relevant?
    - o What's going on in the larger system that might affect your goal or issue and that you need to understand and address?

Once you have answered those questions, you'll have a better idea of which influence skills will be most useful.

Here are a few general principles that can guide you toward success in influencing others:

- Devise a goal involving action you want the other person to take; make sure it's observable during the time you are actively influencing that person. For example, "I want to influence Rae to agree to meet with me once a week for the next three months."

- Balance expressive influence (sending your needs, ideas, offers, and visions to others) with receptive influence (asking for ideas, requirements, concerns, and commitments from others).

- Remember that influence happens in the mind of the other person. Intention and impact are two different things. Focus most of your attention on the other person, not on what you are going to say next.

- Spend time selling your ideas rather than tearing down those of others whom you want to influence. Causing anyone to feel bad, wrong, or stupid guarantees that you won't be able to influence that person.

Julio calls Rae to invite her to meet in a café near the university. When she arrives, he is ready to influence her. "Rae, I'd like you to be part of my team for the next few months.} I have a plan, but having someone to bounce ideas around with will help keep me on track and moving forward."

"You know that I support you and would like to help, but my time is pretty limited," Rae responds.

"You'd like to make sure you don't over-commit, given your other activities."

"Yes, I have a lot to do and many people depending on me."

"What other concerns do you have about this, Rae?"

"I don't want you to depend on me too much; I think you have the ability to move things forward on your own. Actually, I can see you working in your virtual office six months from now with more work than you can handle."

"I think I can make that happen, but I still will need some advice. How about considering a professional exchange?"

"It sounds as if you have something in mind," Rae says.

"I do. How about if I offer to help you manage your money for the next six months in exchange for coaching from you?"

"I have to acknowledge that I'm not very good at that, and I've never employed anyone to help me," Rae says.

"What do you need from me to make that work?"

Rae and Julio end up with an agreement that proves to be satisfying to both of them. Both of them used a variety of influence behaviors, both Expressive and Receptive. Julio has influenced Rae; in return, she has influenced him. Over time, influence is always two-way.

In moving your plan forward, you'll find it necessary to negotiate agreements with others about, for example, participation, resources, timelines, or deliverables. We've discussed some of the behavioral influence skills that might be useful in reaching agreements. You will also want to consider how to manage the process of reaching good agreements.

People often think of negotiation as either a contest where one side wins and the other side loses or a series of compromises where each side ends up with half of what they wanted to gain in the first place. Neither is true or practicable when you are navigating toward an important achievement.

We think of negotiation, instead, as a constructive, collaborative process undertaken by people with differing needs and resources, working together to build an agreement that fulfills all their important needs. It's a project that can be managed rather than an adversarial process. We use the term "constructive negotiation" to refer to a way of building agreement between two or more parties that have some vested interests (something to gain or lose) in conflict and some vested interests in common. A constructive negotiation will result in an exchange of value that meets important needs for all parties and prevents or resolves conflict.

As you navigate your journey, stop from time to time to build these constructive agreements. We liken them to building a shelter—a home or office building that contains and supports certain activities. Starting from the ground up, negotiators establish a solid foundation and move through several phases to build a long-lasting agreement.

Needs drive negotiations; negotiations that fail to fulfill in some way the underlying needs of all parties can't be successful. Important underlying needs, both tangible and intangible, provide the reason to negotiate and the energy for the negotiation. Once these needs are identified, you can begin to plan for your negotiation. A good way to identify these needs in yourself and others is to begin with what you want from the other person or what you believe or understand that he or she might want from you in exchange. Then ask the important question: "What would receiving that do for me and for him or her? What need would it fulfill?" Then ask, "What alternatives exist for meeting that need?" You can list a number of options that each party could offer and that might meet underlying needs.

The essence of negotiation is a fair exchange. You're not seeking the right answer, but rather a fair way of meeting one another's needs, as perceived by both negotiators. Each party must perceive the value of the options exchanged to be roughly equivalent. There are usually a number of alternative options for meeting any need. The most elegant agreements consist of what we call "creative options." These are goods or services of high value to the receiver and low cost to the giver.

If we look at the discussion between Rae and Julio as an informal negotiation, the exchange of consulting services for money management services is an example of an elegant exchange. Both of them offered something they knew how to do in exchange for something they needed to learn about. Negotiation is a process you can manage using your influence skills to accomplish the best possible results for everyone involved. It is all about being fair and creative in finding ways to meet all parties' important needs.

Activities

1. Write down an extended list of potential critical goals for the coming year. Develop a set of criteria to help you select down to the most important ones, then choose two or three critical goals that surface as the most likely to meet all your criteria.

2. Set measures of success for each critical goal and develop a week-by-week tactical plan to achieve each one. Share your commitments with someone who will help you stay on track with them.

3. Consider what external factors might have an impact on the success of your vision—factors that you're not in control of. List these, and then select two or three that are key to the result that you desire. Identify the range of possible outcomes that you can imagine.

4. Develop two or three possible scenarios. Consider how the key factors might play out in each scenario and what you would need to do to succeed or at least survive in each scenario.

5. Draw conclusions from this exercise. Are there actions that would be useful under all three scenarios? How will you know when to take or modify action?

6. List people you need to influence to gain the support or resources you need in the West and the specific action or actions you want each of them to take. What do you know

about each person that will help you to influence him or her more successfully?

7. Choose one of these people, set a near-term influence goal, and decide which of the influence tactics and behaviors might be most useful for a discussion you could have soon. Choose no more than two expressive and two receptive behaviors, and imagine how you might use them for maximum impact.

8. Choose another person who will be key to your success—someone with whom you will need to negotiate for important resources. What needs or vested interests does that person have that you can fulfill as part of an exchange? What options might that person offer that would fulfill your needs?

Chapter 12

The Gaps Model

In this chapter, we will look at the compass to identify and address the gaps you will need to close in your journey to success. Four gaps can occur on this journey:

- the integrity gap

- the execution gap

- the awareness gap, and

- the courage gap.

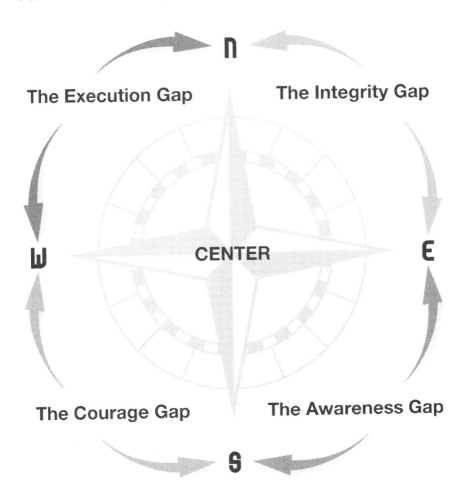

The Integrity Gap

According to this model, internal changes start in the East. There might be a shift of focus in your life or career. There might be a change in circumstances. There might be different values that seem more important at a certain time in your life. When you feel that your current direction is no longer aligned with your internal values and motivations, you experience an integrity gap.

Laura was a respected finance manager leading a team of eight professionals. She had been very good at her role, to which she had been promoted because of a series of successes in the company. Early in the year that I was engaged to coach her, her performance had begun to deteriorate. Reports were incomplete and late; her team complained about Laura's impatience and negative attitude. In the beginning of the self-navigation process, Laura completed a N.E.W.S.™ questionnaire. From the findings of the questionnaire and subsequent conversation, I discovered that her husband of ten years had suddenly left their marriage. This crisis had caused her to reflect on her life and her work.

As we worked together, she observed that she had been a very creative person in her youth and had enjoyed developing elegant solutions to complex problems. She had studied finance and economics because her parents wanted her to take this route and because it offered her a way to generate a comfortable income. At some point in the last year, she had realized that this path was not the right one for her. She realized that she was bored with her role; she felt a deep need to change it. This internal shift motivated her to take part in a number of self-awareness workshops.

After many navigation conversations, Laura started looking for roles in the finance industry that would be more interesting and engage her creative abilities. After the self-navigation process, she found a new position in the mergers and acquisitions department in her company. In this new role, she could learn about many new companies, understand their structure and financial situation, and work out creative ways to merge with them.

Laura had an internal process going on in the East. She felt an integrity gap. Again, this gap occurs when your North is not aligned to your current East. This gap creates a feeling of being in the wrong place, of needing to do something different—to become more aligned with what is important to you. To close the integrity gap, Laura needed to realign her direction, practical model, and vision to her recalibrated East.

The Execution Gap

The next gap that you need to close in your journey to fulfill yourself is the execution gap. This is the gap between your intentions in the North and your actual execution in the West.

Serge was the owner of a medical device company. He was sixty-two at the time I met him. He had worked hard for over thirty years to build the company. Now he felt tired and burned out. He wanted to bring one of his four children in to take his place and lead the company to its next level of development. He would then move to a part-time business-development role, working three days a week to help the company succeed.

This was a very good practical model in the North that was well aligned with Serge's motivations in the East. However, Serge did not manage to execute his plan. The process of bringing one of his children in to manage the company did not work out well; Serge did not take into account his authoritarian management style. He brought his children into the company one after another, but did not provide a well-organized orientation process. Instead, Serge threw them into the deep end and demanded quick results from them without giving them the authority and resources they needed to achieve good outcomes. None of them could succeed in this situation, and they left, one by one. Serge was alone at sixty-five with no successor. On reflection, he realized that he should have asked for help in creating a realistic plan to execute on his intentions.

You can close the execution gap through careful planning and wise translation of your intentions from the North into a practical set of actions in the West. This process of closing gaps—starting from the East and moving first to align your North and then to plan and execute practical actions in the West—can be called the "external arch." You recognize an internal shift, you create a new direction, and then you translate that direction into a well-planned set of actions. If Serge had asked for, received, and listened to some feedback about his pattern of behavior from his children or from a coach, he could have reduced the "blind spot" in his Johari Window, avoided repeating the pattern, and thus increased the likelihood of successful execution.

The Awareness Gap

Similarly, there is an "internal arch" that moves from the East to the South and then back to the West. You feel a desire to change something (East), but as soon as you begin to do something about it, you hit a barrier (South)—perhaps a belief or assumption that stops you from moving to action in the West. The first gap here is the "awareness gap," the gap between the East and the South.

Anita is a young woman from a traditional Asian family that had relocated to the Silicon Valley. Her father was an engineer in a large IT corporation. During our first meeting, Anita looked upset and cried a little from time to time. "They want me to study cooking and work in my uncle's restaurant," she sobbed. "I am too scared to say no, but it isn't something I want to do."

"What are you moved to do as a career? " I asked.

"I can't even think about it. I'm too concerned about what might happen if I refuse to do what my parents want me to do."

"Did you talk to them? Did you express your feelings?"

"Oh, no," she said. "I don't want to disrespect them. They would be very angry at me."

"Before you refuse," I said, "let's explore what really drives you from within. If you discover that, you might gain some clarity and confidence that will allow you to express your wishes."

It turned out that Anita was passionate about children's education, particularly in mathematics. From there, things got easier. She gained the courage to speak to her parents about how she wanted to contribute to society. Being a math teacher was an alternative that her family could respect.

Anita had an awareness gap. Her South was so intense and the voice of her fears was so loud that she was not even aware of her own East, her inner motivation. The navigation process for her was to amplify the sound of that inner voice from the East so that she could become aware of and listen to it through the noisy demons of her South.

The Courage Gap

In the internal arch, we first close the awareness gap and let our true motivation drive us through the barriers in our South. Then we encounter the courage gap. This is the gap between the South and the West. It challenges us to gain the courage to act on our inner decisions and choices.

Matt was a very bright young man, an individual contributor and project leader in a successful start-up company. He loved the work and the technology. He had been employed there since the company started three years earlier. He was in charge of a project that drove the technology innovation of the entire company. Matt's achievements were outstanding, and the company registered six different patents that he created.

Still, Matt felt frustrated. He felt that he was not treated fairly. His boss, the founder of the company, did not recognize his contributions. He never gave him positive feedback. Matt's salary had stayed the same over the last three years, and except for one yearly bonus that all the employees got last year, he did not get anything to reward him for all he had achieved for the company. When I first met Matt, he believed that if he asked for a raise or for stock option, he would lose the job that he loved so much. This was a fierce South.

After a few conversations, Matt became convinced that his skills and talent were worth more than what the company offered him. He also understood that if he lost his job, there would be many other options for him in the industry. He made a choice to break through his South issues and ask his boss for what he felt he deserved.

Week after week, Matt postponed the meeting with his boss, using a variety of excuses. He had a courage gap. He had made a choice and a decision, but he didn't have the courage to act on it. In our meetings, I encouraged Matt, letting him know that I believed he could gain the courage to step out of his South and confront his boss. We rehearsed such a meeting several times until Matt felt that he could do it.

The actual meeting went very well; it turned out that Matt's boss was so preoccupied with funding the company and keeping it going that he had ignored Matt's needs. He was glad that Matt came to him rather than leaving the company for a better offer.

The awareness gap and the courage gap constitute the internal arch that goes from East to South to West. This arch has to do with your internal process of growth—the process of being faithful to your authentic inner drivers in spite of your hesitations and fears. You then find a way to overcome your limits and move toward the actions you know you should take.

Activities

1. Which of the four gaps do you face at this stage in your life and your career?

2. What can you do to close those gaps?

3. What help might you need in order to do it? Who can you call on to support you in this endeavor?

Conclusion

Putting It All Together

We believe that life is all about choice. We face endless choices, and through making them, we create our life and our careers. This is what being human is all about. We are not limited. We live in an open-ended process where we can choose and move beyond our initial limitations.

Choice is not a simple matter. There will always be a question of whether you are making conscious and free choices—using criteria—for your major decisions. As we noted, many of our choices are made by default, based on a "code" that may be outside of our awareness. This is often not to our advantage. Instead, we proposed that you choose according to your authentic passions and core competencies; the authentic "psychic DNA" of your being that should drive your decision making.

As you navigate your life, guided by your internal drivers, you will at times encounter fears or other internal barriers that can stop you from achieving your hopes and dreams. At these moments, you will have a stark choice between giving in to these limitations, fears, and weaknesses or moving toward fulfilling your potential. Many people can help you, but no one can make important, life-changing choices and decisions for you. In a world of ambiguity and constant change, the ability to navigate by making wise choices is a core competence.

The process of navigation requires a navigation system: a compass. In addition, you need a good set of skills and tools. And you can benefit from the stories of those who have made the journey before you.

The stories in this book are of real people we have coached, trained, and accompanied over the many years we both have worked in large and small organizations. We believe that their experience can be of value to you. We hope that this book will help you navigate through the choice points you are currently facing in your life or career and that the N.E.W.S.™ model will become a useful navigation system as you proceed on your journey.

Bon voyage.

B. Kim Barnes
Aviad Goz

Resources

Books

Barnes, B. Kim, *Exercising Influence.* San Francisco: Pfeiffer/Wiley, 2006.

Bennis, W. *On Becoming a Leader.* 4th ed. New York: Basic Books, 2009.

Blanchard, K. *Mission Impossible.* New York: McGraw-Hill, 1999.

Bossidy, L., R. Charan, and C. Burck. *Execution: The Discipline of Getting Things Done.* New York: Crown Business, 2002.

Bridges, William. *Transitions: Making Sense of Life's Changes*, Revised 25th Anniversary Edition, Boston: Da Capo Press, 2004.

Buckingham, M., and C. Coffman. *Now Discover your Strengths.* New York: Free Press, 2001.

Chan, Kim W., and R. Mauborgne. *Blue Ocean Strategy*. Cambridge: Harvard Business School Press, 2005.

Collins, J., and J. I. Porras. *Built to Last: Successful Habits of Visionary Companies*. New York: Harper Business, 2004.

Collins, J. *Good to Great : Why Some Companies Make the Leap…and Others Don't*. New York: Harper Business, 2004.

Collins, J. *How the Mighty Fall: And Why Some Companies Never Give In*. New York: Harper Business, 2009.

Covey, S. R. *The 7 Habit of Highly Effective People*. 15th anniv. ed. New York: Free Press, 2004.

Covey, S. R. *The 8th Habit: From Effectiveness to Greatness*. Running Press Miniature Editions, 2006.

Covey, S. R. *The Speed of Trust: The One thing that Changes Everything*. New York: Free Press, 2006.

De Bono, E., et al. *I Am Right, You Are Wrong: From This to the New Renaissance: From Rock Logic to Water Logic*. London: Penguin, 1992.

Dixit, A. K., and S. Skeath. *Games of Strategy*. 2nd ed. New York: Norton, 2004.

Doz, Y., and M. Kosonen. *Fast Strategy: How Strategic Agility Will Help You Stay Ahead of The Game*. Wharton School Publishing, 2008.

Goz, A., *The Magician from the Judea Desert*. Momentum Group, 1992.

Goz, A., *The Man Who Knew How to Think*. Momentum Group, 1986.

Goz, A., *Results: Your Journey to Personal Effectiveness*. Momentum Group, 1994.

Heath, C., and D. Heath. *Switch: How to Change Things When Change Is Hard*. Crown Business, 2010.

Kaye, B. and J. Giulioni. *Help Them Grow or Watch Them Go: Career Conversations Employees Want.* San Francisco: Berrett-Koehler Publishers, 2012.

Kotter, J. P. *Leading Change.* Cambridge: Harvard Business Press, 1996.

Kouzes, J., and B. Posner. *The Leadership Challenge.* San Francisco: Jossey-Bass, 2008.

Larreche, J. C. *The Momentum Effect.* Philadelphia: Wharton School Publishing, 2009.

Losier, M. J. *Law of Attraction: The Science of Attracting More of What You Want and Less of What You Don't,* Grand Central Life & Style, 2010.

Millman, D. *The Life You Were Born to Live: A Guide to Finding Your Life Purpose.* HJKramer, 1993.

Mintzberg, H., J. Lampel, and B. Ahlstrand. *Strategy Safari.* New York: Free Press, 1998.

Reis, A., and L. Reis. *The 22 Immutable Laws of Branding.* New York: Harper Paperbacks, 2002.

Rodach, G., and H. Besser. *Toutes les clés d'une stratégie Gagnante.* Ed. Sociales Françaises, 2007.

Rodach, G., and A. Goz. *Trouver sa voie.* Esf éditeur, 2009.

Toffler, A., and H. A. Toffler. *War and Anti-War: Making Sense of Today's Global Chaos.* Grand Central Publishing, 1995.

Simon, S., H. Kirschenbaum, and L. Howe. *Values Clarification.* Revised ed., New York: Grand Central Publishing, 1995.

Weihenmayer, E., and P. G. Stoltz. *The Adversity Advantage.* Fireside, 2008.

Wilber, K. *A Brief History of Everything.* 2nd ed. Boston: Shambhala Press, 2007.

Websites

www.newscoaching.com
www.newscoaching.com/blog
www.barnesconti.com
www.aviadgoz.com
www.momentum.org.il
http://strengths.gallup.com/default.aspx

For the full N.E.W.S.™ Questionnaire, visit www.newscoaching.com

Coaching and Training Programs

N.E.W.S.® Coaching and Training:[16]

- Leadership and Executive Coaching

- *The N.E.W.S.™ Experience: Navigating Your Life and Career*

- *Team Navigation: Leading Your Team Toward Success*

- *Organizational Navigation: Leading in an Uncertain World*

- *The Manager as N.E.W.S. Coach*

- *NEWSell: Your Sales Compass for Success*

- *NEWSwalk: An Outdoor Decision-Making Program*

---

16 Copyrighted programs of N.E.W.S.® Coaching and Training.

Barnes & Conti Associates, Inc.[17]

- *Exercising Influence: Building Relationships and Getting Results*

- *Constructive Negotiation: Building Agreements that Work*

- *Managing Innovation: From Strategic Initiative to the Creation of Value* (with David Francis, PhD)

- *Intelligent Risk-taking: From Vision to Action*

- *Strategic Thinking: Leadership Tools for Planning, Problem-solving, and Decision-making*

- *Puzzles, Mysteries, and Muddles: A Problem-Solving Program (with Jerry L. Talley)*

- *The Mastery of Change: Thriving in Interesting Times*

---

17 Copyrighted programs of Barnes & Conti Associates, Inc.

About the Author

B. Kim Barnes is the CEO of Barnes & Conti Associates, Inc., of Berkeley, California. She has over 30 years of experience, as both an internal and external consultant, in the fields of management, leadership, and organization development. Her clients include many global Fortune 100 companies.

Kim is a frequent speaker at professional conferences and has published numerous articles in professional journals and books. She is the primary author of many popular leadership development programs including, among others, *Exercising Influence, Constructive Negotiation, Inspirational Leadership, Intelligent Risk-Taking, Creating a Culture for Innovation, Constructive Debate*, and *Consulting on the Inside*, all copyrighted programs of Barnes & Conti. She co-developed *Managing Innovation: Driving Ideas from Strategic Initiative to Value Creation*, with David Francis, Ph.D., of the University of Brighton's Centre for Research in Innovation Management.

The second edition of her book, *Exercising Influence: A Guide for Making Things Happen at Work, at Home, and in Your Community*, was published by Pfeiffer/Wiley in 2007. *Consulting on the Inside: A Practical Guide for Internal Consultants*, co-authored with Beverly Scott, was published in 2011 by ASTD Press. After completing this book, Kim was inspired to begin writing a tongue-in-cheek corporate mystery series with an internal organizational consultant as the protagonist. The first book of the series, *Murder on the 33rd Floor*, was published in 2012.

For more information about Barnes & Conti's programs, visit www.barnesconti.com

For more information about the Corporate Mystery series, visit www.corporate-mystery.com

About the Author

Aviad Goz

Aviad Goz is a respected leader in the field of personal and organizational development. He is the Founder and Chairman of the Momentum Group as well as the founder and Chief Visionary Officer of N.E.W.S.®Coaching and Training, based in Lausanne, Switzerland. He has presented seminars and coached executives in Fortune 100 companies across the globe. He has special expertise in organizational navigation, leadership development, and executive coaching and is a popular speaker on these topics in many venues. His background includes the life sciences, psychobiology and behavioral science.

Aviad is the developer of unique training and coaching approaches, such as the N.E.W.S.™ navigation model and many programs that apply that model to individual growth as well as team and organizational leadership. Using that model, he and his business partner, Laurent Choppe, have successfully developed a company that is now active in 23 countries. He travels around the globe, teaching seminars and coaching leaders, for much of the year.

Aviad has coached hundreds of CEOs, executives, business owners, artists, and public figures. He has been an international seminar leader since 1986, and has trained participants in over 1500 companies in 50 different countries. Among his clients are many Fortune 100 companies in Europe, Asia, and the Americas.

Aviad has authored or co-authored eight books in Hebrew, English and French. He has published dozens of articles in human resources, organization development, and medical journals. His most recent books include "Trouvez sa voie," co-authored with Gerard Rodach and "Life of Joy," co-authored with Roni Ratner.

For more information about the Momentum Group, visit www.momentum.org.il

For more information about N.E.W.S.™, visit www.newscoaching.com

Made in the USA
Charleston, SC
11 February 2013